71.38

R4.00

64.25

11.00

R321.50

2.00

R343.13

43.90°

100.38

53.75

12.13

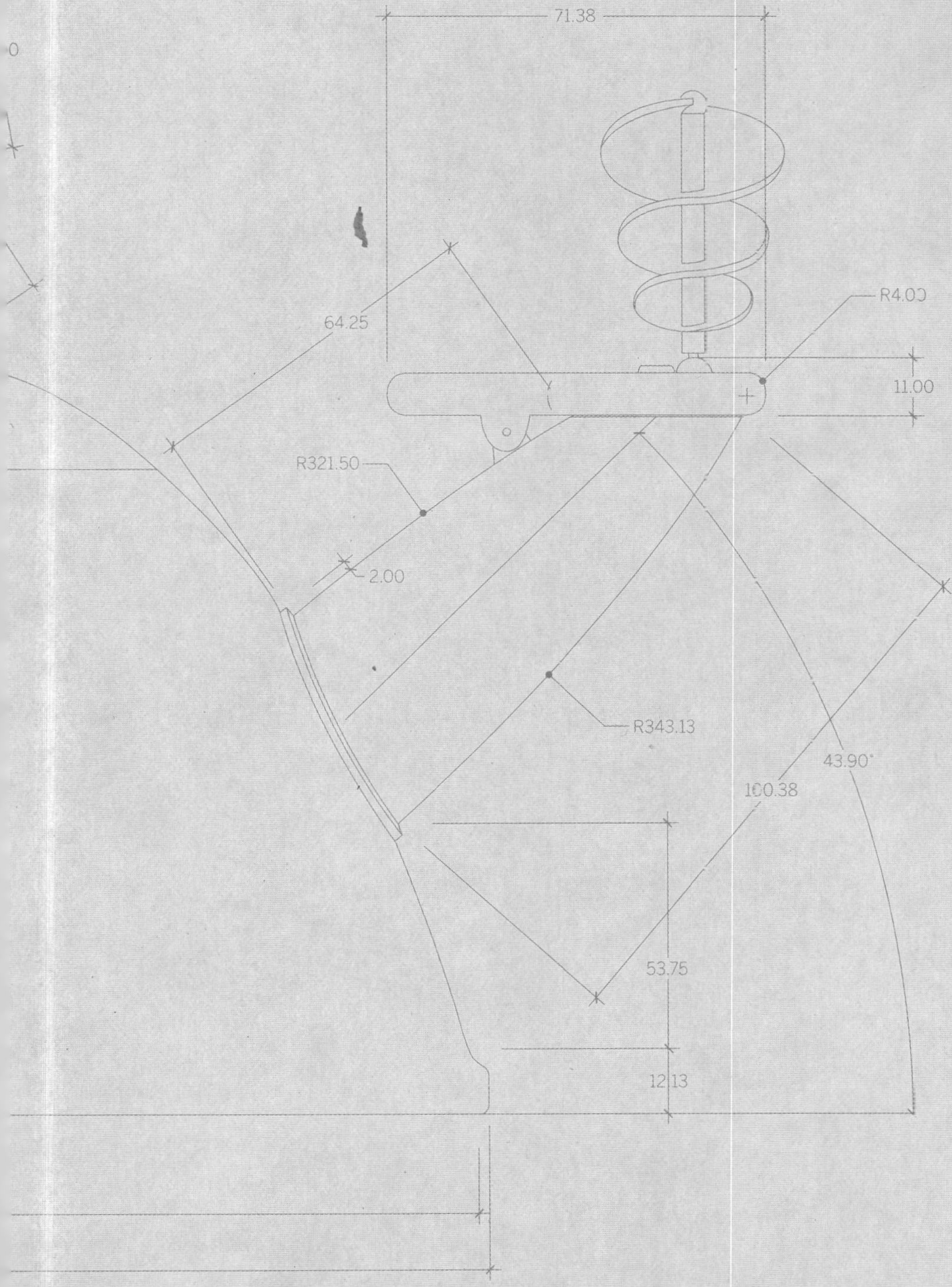

VIEW

Michael Graves Designs

The Art of the Everyday Object

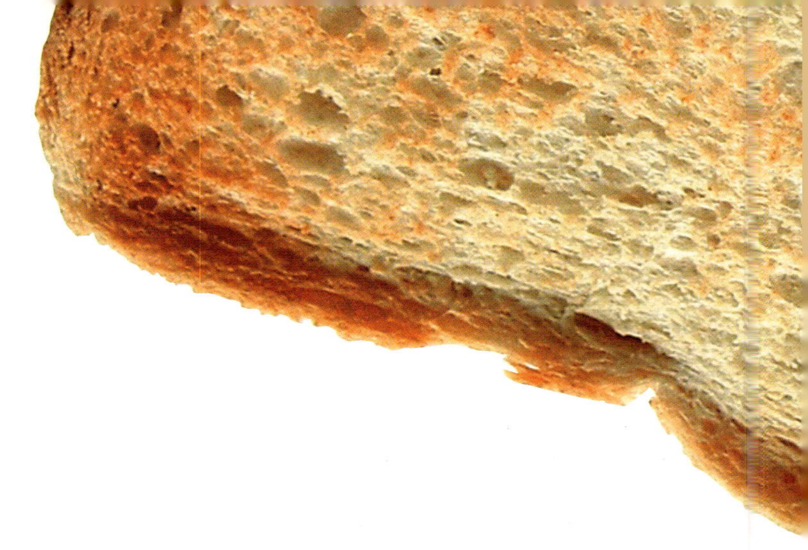

Michael Graves
The Art of the Eve

by Phil Patton

with
Michael Graves
Design Group

MELCHER
MEDIA

Designs

yday Object

This book was produced by
Melcher Media, Inc.
124 West 13th Street, New York, NY 10011
Publisher: Charles Melcher
Editor in Chief: Duncan Bock
Project Editor: Elizabeth Johnson
Publishing Manager: Bonnie Eldon
Editorial Assistant: Lauren Nathan
Production Director: Andrea Hirsh

Library of Congress Control Number:
2004100965

Design by Pentagram

Printed in China

ISBN: 0-9717935-2-2

10 9 8 7 6 5 4 3 2 1

Below: Wristwatch for Target, 2000

Opposite: Kitchen timer for Alessi, 1993

Contents

The offices of Michael Graves are located in two former houses across the street from one another: architecture in the brick structure (left) and product design in the wooden building (right).

Introduction

Two large yellow houses face each other on Nassau Street in Princeton, New Jersey. One, built of brick, dates from the eighteenth century and has been, by turns, an inn, a brothel, and a girls' school. The other, of a similar shape but made of wood, was built in the nineteenth century. A hundred and fifty years ago, the street between them was the well-traveled route carrying horsemen and carriages between New York and Philadelphia.

Today the houses contain the offices of Michael Graves' architectural and product design firms and represent the site of one of the most remarkable aesthetic experiments of our time. Inside, his firm has created plans for private homes and public buildings, including the iconic, light-filled Denver Central Library and two exuberant hotels at Walt Disney World in Florida that are crowned with giant swans and dolphins. His architecture makes the user's experience the most important concern—a rarity in the field. It is a distinctly humane and livable architecture unlike the work of any of his contemporaries.

Visitors often remark about the "Santa's workshop" quality of Graves' design studios.

Left: The design staff works in studios or teams, each of which handles multiple projects at once.

Right: Color is an essential aspect of Graves' design work in architecture, interiors, and products. In addition to consulting the firm's in-house artist, who develops custom color strategies in paint form, the designers utilize various standard systems to select color palettes.

More radically, Graves has brought the same generous democratic spirit to household objects as common as forks and toilet brushes. Already established as one of the most important architects of the era, Graves has created a new practice since the 1980s, designing products that have not only transformed the American home but have helped to change Americans' view of design in general. He helped realize a goal at least a century old—bringing beautiful products to the ordinary home and office. Graves first ventured into this territory through his architectural practice, when he designed custom furniture and lighting for his early buildings. He went on to create luxury goods for Alessi, Steuben, Swid Powell, and other companies before revolutionizing products for the popular market in an alliance with Target and its more than twelve hundred stores. Today, his firm has designed more than fifteen hundred products for its clients, with combined sales exceeding $100 million annually. This work, which includes humble kitchen spatulas and pencil cups, has earned Graves praise from no less a figure than President Bill Clinton.

Graves has long believed that the quality of the things we use and surround ourselves with, like the buildings we live and work in, affect human souls. His is a generous and humanistic approach that links him with sources as varied as the Renaissance, the Bauhaus, and the Arts and Crafts movement. "If you want a golden rule that will fit everybody," declared English designer William Morris in 1880, "this is it: Have nothing in your houses that you do not know to be useful, or believe to be beautiful."

Mailbox (designed for Projects, 1990) located at the entrance to the Graves Design Studio Store

Left: Michael Graves at work in his drafting studio

Below, left to right:

Assortment of clocks for Target

The Graves Design Studio Store merchandised with Graves' private-label and licensed collections of clocks, frames, glassware, jewelry, and wristwatches, incuding many items designed for Alessi

Wristwatches designed for Projects (1993–98), Fantasma for the Walt Disney Company (1992), FAO Schwarz (1994), and Pierre Junod (2003)

Many architects design and build their own offices as statements of their philosophy and style. In adapting the two Princeton houses for his practice, Graves made another kind of statement. He was working inside history, innovating from within tradition. Modernism had wanted to sweep away history; postmodernism had used it as a source from which to clip and paste. Graves, however, wanted to become part of history—and add to it.

In the large brick building, which houses the architectural practice, plans and drawings cover the walls of the warren of offices. Models of buildings and objects cluster on tables. Dogs—retrievers, shepherds, and a poodle—wander the halls. The current alpha male answers to the name of Bauhaus.

The product design division is headquartered in the wood-frame building. In rooms where people once lived and slept, two dozen designers work at computers. Jammed closely together, these young people dream up next year's kitchen tools, office accessories, and cordless phones. The mood is one of quiet activity, a gentle buzz. Visitors often remark about the "Santa's workshop" quality of the place. The creation of innovative, modern tools within such a traditional building suggests the highly personal nature of Michael Graves and his work.

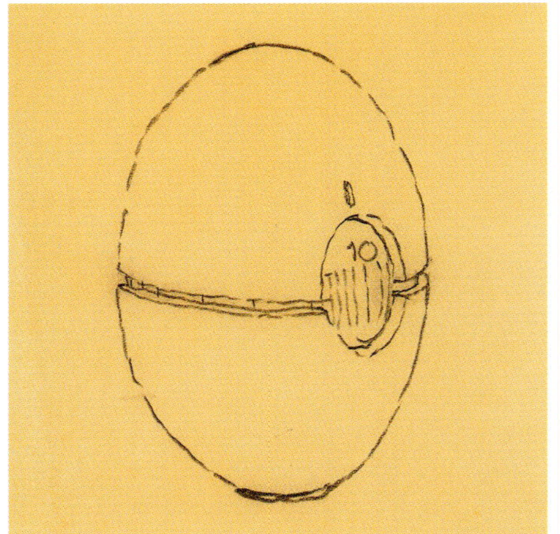

The oval theme of Graves' products for Target—obvious in the egg timer—was more subtly echoed in items for the garden: furniture, flower pots, tools, gloves, and a watering can.

The classic corded black telephone that debuted at Target (2000) shared an affinity with objects from industrial design's heroic era, such as Bell Telephone's "Model 302" (1937), designed by Henry Dreyfuss (below).

Stuck to some of the computer monitors are Post-it–sized sketches in Graves' familiar hatched and outlined style. Not all effects are directly work-related. A tiny windup toy sits here, a Hot Wheels car there. One designer looks toward a framed snapshot of a man in uniform who looks just like him. It is his twin brother, serving in the Middle East.

What's more, no other firm has what Graves installed on the ground floor: a retail shop. Founded in 1994, the Graves Design Studio Store sells the fruits of the elves' labor—teakettles and coffee pots, clocks and watches, frames and lamps, leather goods and china. It recalls the place of business of an old-time craftsman who lived above his workshop, and its varied contents suggest why Graves has won not only the National Medal of Arts and the American Institute of Architects' highest honor, the Gold Medal, but also awards from the Industrial Designers Society of America.

Although it has been converted into an office, the place still feels like a house—a space not just for working but for living. Rather than the impersonal cubicles of most architectural and design firms, Graves' young associates work in converted bedrooms and dining rooms—a conceit that makes perfect sense for this firm. At the root of their work, binding together the architecture and product design, lies the idea of domesticity. No idea is more fundamental to this practice. Graves sees domesticity not only in architecture but in paintings and products. It crosses artificial artistic distinctions between "high" and "low." "The quality of 'domesticity' combines an interest in culture with the design of physical artifacts," Graves says. Belief in the importance of the ordinary person led Graves to value the ordinary object.

As a designer, Graves likes to call himself a "general practitioner"—suggesting not a specialist, a brain surgeon or orthopedist, but a family doctor who may even make house calls. In an age of specialists, there are few general designers. "As an architect," he says, "I never understood why I had to stop at the door."

The conference room in the Graves product design offices is lined with shelves filled with decades of models, prototypes, and finished products for approximately fifty different companies. Above the table is a Graves-designed chandelier for Baldinger Architectural Lighting.

Graves' design philosophy grew out of the industrial revolution. The introduction of mass production in the nineteenth century meant that household items and tools were no longer made one at a time by hand; factories greatly reduced both the time and money required for making ordinary objects. A revolution in aesthetics soon followed. European artists and designers created a new machine-age look that reflected the new manufacturing processes. They imagined every home filled with elegant, affordable pieces, from furniture to drinking glasses. They founded workshops and schools devoted to this new way of designing—most notably, the Wiener Werkstätte (Viennese Workshops) in 1903 and the Bauhaus in Germany in 1919. In the 1930s, known as the "heroic" age of American industrial design, such figures as Walter Dorwin Teague, Henry Dreyfuss, and Raymond Loewy boasted of being able to design everything "from a lipstick to a locomotive."

Around the same time, architects and designers consciously sought to make their work relevant to the middle class. Frank Lloyd Wright's Usonian houses and Russel Wright's modern dinnerware were both designed to meet modest household budgets. Both Wrights believed that design could be functional without becoming abstract, that it could be as witty as comic books and as entertaining as film. Graves' work, especially for the discount retailer Target, continues this tradition, forgotten in the years between, of uniting mass production and high design.

But this tradition also has a far more powerful, earlier model: the Renaissance. Graves' reputation as "a Renaissance man" is not off-mark. He is well aware of the belief of Renaissance humanists that nothing human is beneath one's view. Artists and architects in sixteenth-century Italy were not yet specialized. Graves likes to point to Michelangelo, painter, sculptor, architect, planner of city squares and aristocratic mausoleums, but also designer of fortifications and theatrical sets—and even, according to legend, the uniforms of the Swiss Guard, the Papal security force. But Graves' range of projects—campuses and libraries, chairs and coffeepots, brooms and garlic presses—extends even further.

Graves challenges the notion of a hierarchy of design: he applies the same effort to chairs and toasters that he does to elements of a hotel or a corporate headquarters. The result has made Americans think twice about the smallest objects in their homes, even soap dishes and vegetable peelers. For all the ebullience and abundance of industry and the sometimes extreme displays of luxury that the United States has produced over two centuries, beauty has often been neglected. Cradled in Puritanism and matured in the hardships of the frontier, American culture, unlike its European or Asian counterparts, had rarely paused to admire the importance of the ordinary object. Graves has been an instrumental figure in a recent revolution in taste. Whereas shoppers used to be satisfied with a simple signature on a pair of jeans or a label on bedsheets, they are now aware of the aesthetic and functional possibilities of the most commonplace objects. For the general public, design has become a quality that can be found—or missed—in every aspect of life. ■

Opposite: Michelangelo's diverse interests included household objects such as the candleholder he imagined in 1535 (*Design for a Candelabrum*). Brooks Stevens' sporty and fashionable Petipoint iron, produced by the Northwestern Manufacturing Company in 1941, exemplifies the Streamlined style with its swooping aerodynamic lines.

Below: Mantel clock for Projects, 2001

Princeton by Way of Italy and Indiana

Michael Graves was born in 1934 in Indiana, and he has often recalled that as a child, "I was good at drawing and at not much else." When he declared his desire to be an artist, his mother warned, "If you are not as good as Picasso, you will starve." She suggested that he become either an engineer or an architect instead. He didn't know what either profession did, but when he learned the definition of engineering, he immediately decided on architecture and turned his pen to drawing houses in the neighborhood.

Graves came to understand drawing not just as a means of representing things but as a mode of thinking, a medium of inventing and exploring ideas.

Mrs. Graves neglected to mention another profession then enjoying popularity in the United States: industrial designer. Pioneers of this new field, such as Raymond Loewy (who introduced slanted windshields and built-in headlights on automobiles and designed the Lucky Strike cigarette logo) and Henry Dreyfuss (creator of the Trimline phone and the classic circular thermostat for Honeywell), fascinated a country mired in the Depression. They added flair to products that were once simply functional, creating continuous demand and, in the eyes of the companies that hired them, stimulating sales with style.

In 1934, the year of Graves' birth, the Century of Progress Exposition in Chicago welcomed the Streamlined aluminum train called the Zephyr.

Michael Graves receiving the National Medal of Arts from President Bill Clinton, 1999

Industrial designers created visions of the future, turning drawings into reality that was then displayed at the world's fairs of the decade. They rounded and streamlined not only automobiles and locomotives, but also ordinary household products, attempting to bring excitement and speed to a dull, sluggish economy. They worked closely with companies. General Motors had hired Harley Earl from Hollywood to create the departments of Art and Color, and later Styling, to provide variety and luxury for the middle classes with such cars as the 1934 LaSalle. Earl's designs were themselves like Hollywood films—flashy and bright, crafted to bring visions of grandeur to Main Street. Industrial designers looked to the examples provided by Earl, GM, and Detroit's other carmakers as they created new models of household appliances and tools each year.

The year of the LaSalle also saw the peak of the Streamlined style, exemplified by the Chrysler Airflow sedan and the Burlington Zephyr train. Toasters, refrigerators, and radios were appearing in dizzying variety, decorated with sweeping bands of chrome and bright colors. Buildings were not immune, especially those devoted to modern transportation—most notably, Cincinnati's Union

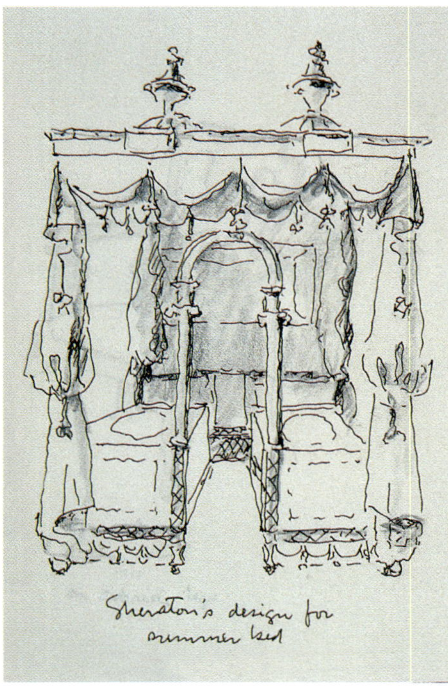

Graves has drawn daily since he was a child. Dozens of sketchbooks constitute a virtual diary of his thinking and observing, including a sketch of an Ingres painting of the so-called *House of Raphael* (above) and Sheraton's buildinglike design for a summer bed (left).

Opposite: George Nelson, Ball clock, 1948

Terminal railroad station, with its vast curving profile and outstretched arms, opened in 1933. Art Deco evolved toward the *moderne* rather than the modern.

The modern was still a European idea of functional, geometrical design, promoted by the Museum of Modern Art in its 1934 show *Art of the Machine*, which celebrated the design of the engineered: ball bearings, propellers, and lab flasks. By contrast, Americans needed product variety as a means to express status and individuality at once, and industrial designers provided the way. Mass production and mass distribution had helped define the American dream as one of low-cost goods for the many. Indeed, Sears, Roebuck and Montgomery Ward catalogs were called "dream books." These catalogs were avidly perused across the United States, with orders fulfilled by the railroads and rural free delivery, which brought goods from factories and warehouses to the distant farms and villages of the heartland. No wonder Franklin Roosevelt said that the best way to fight communism would be to drop Sears catalogs into the Soviet Union.

While the Midwest was being Streamlined, Graves' high school teachers had to invent new drawing classes after he finished the ones they offered. He came to understand drawing not just as a means of representing things but as a mode of thinking, a medium of inventing and exploring ideas.

Graves studied architecture at the University of Cincinnati. It was a co-op program with a six-year degree. "I would spend two months in class, then two months working in an architecture office," he recalls. As a result, Graves not only learned architectural theory and history, but also gained hands-on experience with blueprints and the nuts and bolts of construction. This education was unlike that of many ivory tower architects, who do not find an opportunity to build until late in their careers, and then often have difficulty converting plans born in theory into steel, concrete, bricks, and drywall.

He went on to study at the Harvard Graduate School of Design, which was still strongly influenced by its recent chair, Walter Gropius, the former director of the Bauhaus, who had made Harvard a center of modernist thinking in the U.S. After receiving his master's degree in 1959, Graves worked for a brief time in the office of designer George Nelson, famed for his tables and sofas for Herman Miller and his playful Atomic and Ball clocks. Graves worked on residential architecture for Nelson,

Left: One of Graves' first built projects was an addition to the Benacerraf House, Princeton, New Jersey, designed in 1969.

Below: Graves won the commission for the award-winning Portland Building, the municipal headquarters of Portland, Oregon, through an international design competition that was judged in 1980.

and during this period he admired the work of Alexander Girard, who brought color to Herman Miller, and Russel Wright, whose department store china was one of the first popularly accessible lines of what would later be called "lifestyle" products.

But Graves also saw architects stepping away from the design of furniture and other items that had come naturally to the modernist pantheon of Mies van der Rohe, Le Corbusier, Marcel Breuer, Frank Lloyd Wright, and so many others. And the Bauhaus ideal of products, like buildings, that used modern industrial methods to lower costs to affordable levels fell away. Product design sank in prestige. Edgar Kaufmann of the Museum of Modern Art castigated industrial designers as mere stylists, applying false aerodynamic forms to static objects, and the reputations of figures like Raymond Loewy suffered. A gap soon opened up between architecture and product design.

The award-winning Humana corporate headquarters, in Louisville, Kentucky (1982), uniquely reflects its surroundings. The lower portion is scaled to the neighborhood's nineteenth-century cast-iron rowhouses, and the tower holds its own against the modern building next door. The steel trusses supporting the bowed upper-level terrace are reminiscent of the bridges crossing the Ohio River, visible from the site.

In 1960 Graves won the coveted Rome Prize and spent two years at the American Academy in Rome. Like Louis Kahn, Robert Venturi, and other important architects who had formative experiences while in residence at the Academy, Graves found that his time there had a profound effect on his outlook. "I learned the nouns and verbs and adjectives of architecture there," he recalls. If architecture had a language, this was it: the timeless grammar of base, middle, and top; the beginning, middle, and end of the story, told by a design. In Italy, too, he encountered figures like Gio Ponti, who was as famous for his Superleggera chair as for his Pirelli skyscraper. Designing buildings and other products, from Olivetti typewriters to Pavoni espresso machines, was still a single profession in Italy.

When Graves returned to the United States, he began teaching at Princeton University in 1962 and set up his own architectural practice, on the side, in 1964. There were few jobs and they were small, mostly residences in Indiana and New Jersey, which Graves designed as white, planar cubes. By 1969, Graves' ideas and work had gained sufficient attention to earn him inclusion in *Five Architects*, a conference held at the

Graves designed every detail of the Humana Building inside and out, down to the custom light fixtures that became the basis of his collections for Baldinger Architectural Lighting.

Museum of Modern Art documenting current work of the so-called New York Five: Peter Eisenman, Richard Meier, John Hejduk, Charles Gwathmey, and Graves. At the time, all five were known for austere, white, modernist forms and were sometimes called "The Whites."

In the same period, new ideas, the germs of what was to become known as postmodernism—a term Graves despises—were in the air. Architects and the public alike gained a new appreciation for historic buildings. The historic preservation movement was born in 1963, when McKim, Mead & White's neoclassical palace of transportation, New York's Penn Station, was torn down to make way for a new building. Around the same time, two important books, Jane Jacobs' *The Death and Life of Great American Cities* (1961) and architect Robert Venturi's *Complexity and Contradiction in Architecture* (1966), defined the shortcomings of modernism—namely, that modern buildings, with their vast size and stark exteriors, failed to address tradition, the neighborhoods in which they were built, and the ordinary person in the street. By contrast, a new style of architecture, postmodernism, sought to restore a sense of tradition and continuity, and to make architecture less somber and more understandable to the public. Instead of faceless skyscrapers on huge concrete plazas, postmodernists designed buildings with, among other things, cornices, window moldings, and human-scaled entries. Throughout the 1970s and early 1980s, the field of architecture was dominated by the debate between modernists and postmodernists, and Graves' thinking evolved. He began to stake out his own ground, between the two rival camps, by applying the architectural "language" he had learned in Italy to his designs, and his work changed dramatically.

By the beginning of the 1980s, Graves had arrived at a new sort of synthesis, which brought him his first large commissions and much praise from the architecture community. His public services building in Portland, Oregon (1980–82), and the Humana corporate headquarters in Louisville, Kentucky (1982–85), merged human scale at the ground with an overall public presence. The Portland building was an unabashed glorification of civic virtues and, divided into base, shaft, and capital, it suggested a classical column at huge scale. The proportions of the Humana building reflected the structures of the city's neighboring nineteenth-century cast-iron structures. Its

exterior features—with a bowed upper balcony supported by a truss and a waterfall inside the entrance loggia—alluded to Louisville's bridges and the adjacent Ohio River. In cities populated with monochromatic skyscrapers, both the Portland and Humana buildings used color as well as the design itself to break the exteriors down into parts that hint at the functions within.

With Humana, Graves reversed then current architectural trends and designed the building's interiors as well as the exteriors, granting the building an aesthetic cohesion. He concentrated on the "feeling" of rooms, particularly the public spaces, and ways they were affected by scale. Details, ornament, and fixtures became important elements in perfecting the sense of a space, leading Graves to think about designing lighting and furniture. Frank Lloyd Wright had famously created lighting and furniture, either built-in or designed to match, in many of his best-known buildings, and Graves was well aware of the early modernist tenet that one person should design the things in a building as well as the building itself. The masters of early modernism in Vienna such as Josef Hoffmann conceived of a building and its interior as a *Gesamtkunstwerk* (complete work of art), radiating a single vision, a single hand, and a single mood. In a variation on the idea, Graves believed that designers should be willing to take on small products as well as large projects.

In designing Humana's interiors, he found that many of the elements he desired were not available, so he designed custom lighting fixtures, such as wall sconces and hanging pendant lights. Evoking the Art Deco era in bronze and frosted glass, they stood out in contrast to the recessed can lights and fluorescent tubes that lit so many newly constructed office buildings. Graves forged relationships with such companies as Baldinger Architectural Lighting and later arranged for some of these items to be made in greater quantities for sale to architects and interior designers. These pieces represent some of his first forays into product design for a limited but nonetheless public market.

A series of showrooms for the Sunar (later SunarHauserman) furniture company (Dallas, 1982) created opportunities for a broad range of architectural experimentation and raised Graves' hopes for a furniture collection of his own. Among the few pieces Sunar produced in limited editions were a lounge chair (1982) and a side chair (1981).

Around the same time as these first major architectural breakthroughs, Graves completed the first of his numerous showrooms for furniture maker Sunar (later SunarHauserman). What intrigued Graves about the project, however, was the chance, as he saw it, to design furniture as well as the rooms in which to display it. He asked, and Sunar agreed. Done in the same fertile period as the Portland and Humana buildings, the Sunar designs coincided with the maturation of Graves' thinking about design as a symbolic language.

His first tables and side and lounge chairs appeared around 1980 and, in the following years, were sold by custom order. Made of bird's-eye maple with black accents, the Sunar chairs and tables echoed the neoclassical style and a relatively obscure style called Biedermeier. Long derided by tastemakers, Biedermeier was itself a novel pastiche of historical styles. Born in nineteenth-century Germany, it alluded to both an earlier French style and the forms of ancient Greece. It became the embodiment of bourgeois comfort in Germany and Austria from 1815 to 1850. During that time the luxuries previously restricted to the aristocracy were being sold in less ornate form and in lower-value materials to the rising bourgeoisie. Biedermeier was a style built around comfort, even coziness, in the domestic sphere. By picking up on it, Graves added another layer to its striations of history—and a reminder that history was itself a sequence of recollections of history. Although Graves' Sunar furniture did not catch on in large numbers, it was memorable. Not coincidentally, it was soon after these first product design ventures that Graves was visited by the Italian manufacturer Alberto Alessi regarding a teakettle that was to revolutionize design. ■

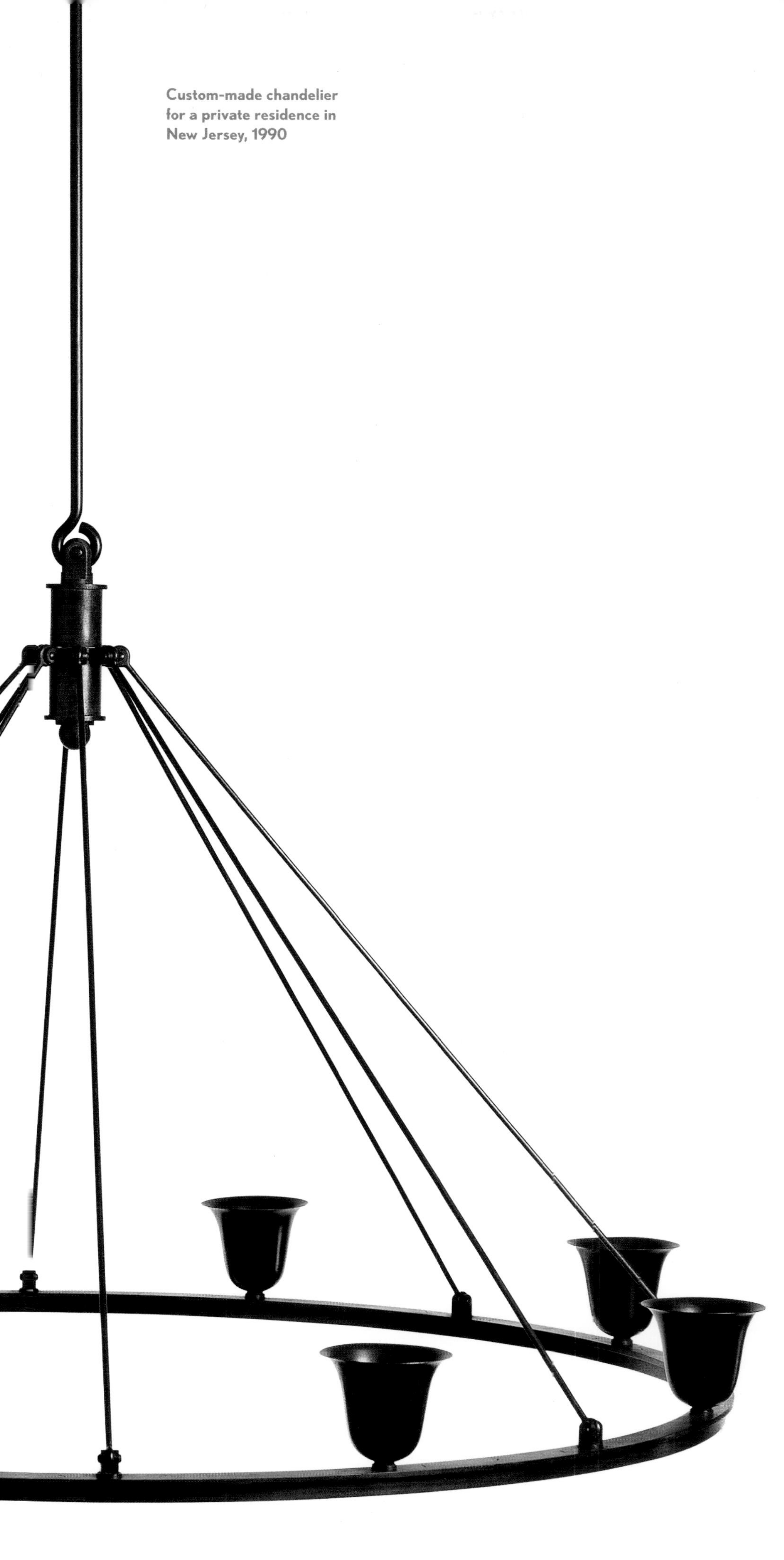

Custom-made chandelier for a private residence in New Jersey, 1990

Michael Graves on **Figurative Design**

Mantel clock for Alessi, 1986

My design practice—in both architecture and consumer products—has been an ongoing investigation of a language of forms that express the myths and rituals of our culture. Years ago, I coined the phrase "figurative architecture" to describe my buildings. By extension, "figurative design" characterizes the way my products embrace similar humanistic concerns. I believe that people make natural associations with forms (as well as with materials and colors). Forms that are familiar and accessible can convey meaning because we associate with them. This interest in figurative design counterbalances the modern preference for abstraction, but I don't think the figurative and the abstract are mutually exclusive.

For much of the twentieth century, the prevalent design aesthetic was based on geometry and abstraction. This aesthetic evolved from early modern fascination with technology, with the machine and its metaphors. Computers have created an interest in abstraction. For years, "good design" in both architecture and products was synonymous with "modern," which translated as "abstract." However, I personally find some modern buildings alienating. The iden-

tity of their elements—even components as basic as walls, windows, and doors—is not perceptible. Constructs such as "window walls" subvert the language and strike me as architectural slang. Some modern objects have become so abstract as to be obscure, to the point where you don't know what they are or which end to pick up. My own design goals are to create familiar, figurative forms while also drawing on the lessons of modern composition. I want the design language to be understandable but not simplistic, and what I learned from modernism helps to make that happen. The poet Wallace Stevens once made a comment to the effect that you have to be literal enough to get the reader into the text and abstract enough to keep him there. This is also the way I view a composer like Mozart. You can enjoy Mozart's music right away, you can hum it, but upon closer investigation you can also discover more and more. In designing everyday objects, I want to encourage the impression of familiarity and also allow those objects to be seen in a slightly different way. Even useful objects can have symbolic function as well as a pragmatic one. In achieving these goals, we often combine simple utility, functional innovation, and formal beauty.

Denver Central Library (1990) rotunda detail (above) and Western History Reading Room (right)

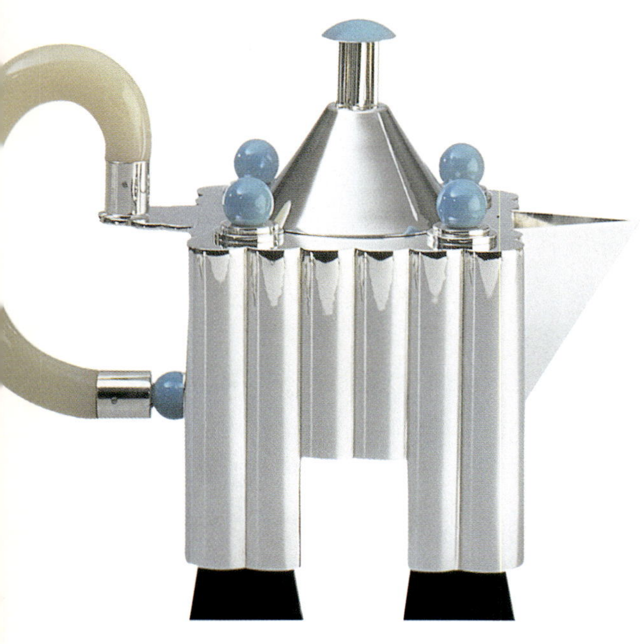

The Teakettle Elevated: Alessi

Graves' first wide acclaim for product design came in the 1980s for work he did for the Italian firm Alessi. Established in 1921 to make metal products, Alessi is known for tabletop and kitchen items. It is located in Crusinallo in the mountainous Strona Valley of Italy, for centuries a center of skilled metalworkers. Many of the company's original objects are still in production.

Alessi came to see Graves as the human embodiment of American commerce—and perhaps as the key to the large sales in the U.S. that his firm had desired but never achieved.

Since the early 1970s, Alessi has been under the direction of Alberto Alessi, the third generation to run the company. Under his watch, the firm has recruited the finest designers from around the world to create new directions for household objects. Alessi began by enlisting the renowned Italian designer Ettore Sottsass. A few years later, Alessi reached out to Richard Sapper, a German practicing in Italy, who in 1979 created an iconic teakettle with a train whistle spout that caught the attention of other designers.

Opposite: Sterling silver teapot for Alessi's Tea and Coffee Piazza program, 1983

Right: Over two million units of Graves' whistling bird teakettle for Alessi have been sold since its introduction in 1985.

Below: Richard Sapper's 1979 teakettle for Alessi used a railroad whistle.

Following the success of Sapper's teakettle, Alessi and his consultant, the postmodern architect Alessandro Mendini, launched a project—the Tea and Coffee Piazza program—to publicize the company and push the commercial envelope of design. In 1980, they invited eleven noted architects to design tabletop sets in which the tray would serve as "the piazza" (or square), and the pots, the buildings. The architects were Hans Hollein, Charles Jencks, Richard Meier, Paolo Portoghesi, Aldo Rossi, Stanley Tigerman, Oscar Tusquets, Robert Venturi, Kazumasa Yamashita, Mendini himself, and Graves. The project literalized the phrase "domestic landscape," derived from the title of a landmark 1972 show at the Museum of Modern Art in New York called *Italy: The New Domestic Landscape*. Each resulting piazza set was offered in 1983 in a maximum edition of ninety-nine, made to order through the Max Protetch Gallery in New York. Graves' contribution was a set of sterling silver vessels that, in their architectonic forms, including square shapes and fluted walls, resemble columns with bases and tops. More successful as design than as retail products, most of the eleven sets sold only a handful of units. Graves', however, sold about twenty-five, he recalls, at a price of $25,000 each.

While the Alessi sets were being shown at museums around the U.S., Graves was invited to the White House. After dinner, Nancy Reagan led him on a tour of the pantry where the White House china and silver were stored. Following the impromptu tour, she requested that he donate one of his Tea and Coffee Piazzas to the White House. Graves explained that he could not afford to make the donation, but he would ask Alessi. Less than sympathetic to the Reagan administration, Alberto Alessi declined.

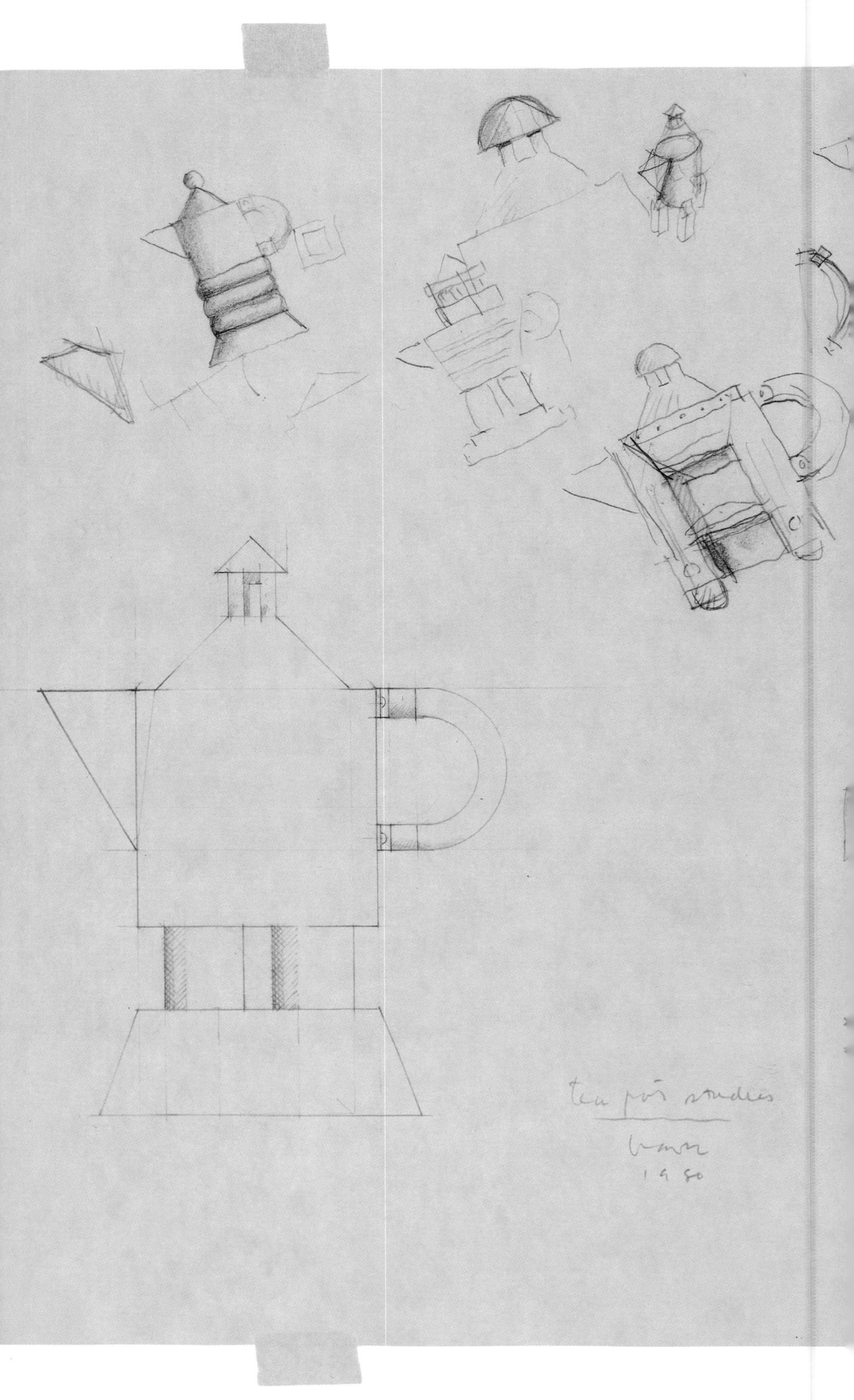
tea pot studies
1980

Studies for the Alessi Tea and Coffee Piazza program, 1980

Below: Olive oil can for Alessi, 2002

Right: Demitasse cup, saucer, and spoon for Alessi, 1989

Bottom right: Pelicano espresso maker, 1996

Following pages: Graves' whistling bird teakettles in production at the Alessi factory in Crusinallo, near Milan, Italy

Alessi came to see Graves as the human embodiment of American commerce—and perhaps the key to the large sales in the U.S. that his firm had desired but never achieved. "Perhaps like no other designer I worked with in the 1980s, Graves has shown that he is able to fascinate the general public," Alberto Alessi once said. "His gift is an incredible capacity to tune in to public taste. It appears to be a natural instinct."

The Tea and Coffee Piazza series led to Alessi's Officina line, including teapots and coffeepots—again designed by various world-famous architects and again imagined as buildings. The original launch included Aldo Rossi's espresso makers, with conical "cupolas" and rounded "domes," and Graves' soon-to-be-famous kettle. The teakettle with its bird-shaped whistle appeared in 1985 and has since become Alessi's most popular product, having sold more than two million units.

Remembering how he set about designing the teakettle, Graves says, "There were real functional constraints to the kettle. Alessi wanted a kettle that would heat quickly and therefore one with a large bottom, without making the handle too hot to touch." This requirement was a response to criticism of Richard Sapper's kettle. Graves insulated the handle to keep it cool and indicated this consideration to the user with a cool blue-gray. The bird on the spout that lends the kettle its charm is a kind of hood ornament, but it also functions as the whistle. Its red color evokes a rooster. "I grew up in Indiana," Graves says, "where we really did get up to the sound of the rooster in the morning. I initially thought of the teakettle as the red rooster and wanted to name it *gallo rosso*, which is Italian for red rooster."

Since its launch, Graves' kettle has become an iconic representation of an era when architects were suddenly being called on to design everything from watches to cups to doghouses. Seen in a kitchen—as in the movie *Ransom*—it immediately told a savvy viewer something about the social and economic status of the owner. But the original idea had been to create an affordable product that would put Alessi on the wider radar screen in the United States. "They asked me how much I thought the teakettle should cost to sell in America," Graves recalls. "I said, 'About what a Revereware kettle costs.' They put it out at $125. That was not what we had in mind." Nevertheless, the price did not seem to hurt sales.

The extensive Dreamscape bath collection (2000)—manufactured by three German companies, Duravit, Dornbracht, and Hoesch—included pedestal and wall-mounted sinks, bathtubs, toilets, bidets, cabinets, hardware, and accessories. The ad campaign featured ephemeral butterflies, evoking the collection's fantastical qualities.

What Graves wanted was different. Much as he enjoyed the fame of the teakettle, he did not want to create products that were desirable simply for their status, as symbols of the owner's taste or success. He wanted products that sold not in spite of their price, but because of their value—in other words, because of their price and design at once.

The problem with the style that became popularly known as postmodernism was that while it recognized the need for a figurative language and a relation to the past, Graves believed that it too often simply quoted the past. It treated history as a storehouse of images to be rifled through for citation, rather than as a continuum of experience. Graves' own take on history was different. He became interested in a whole range of design precedents—from the classical to the neoclassical, as well as the Art Deco and Streamlined Moderne he had grown up with in Indiana.

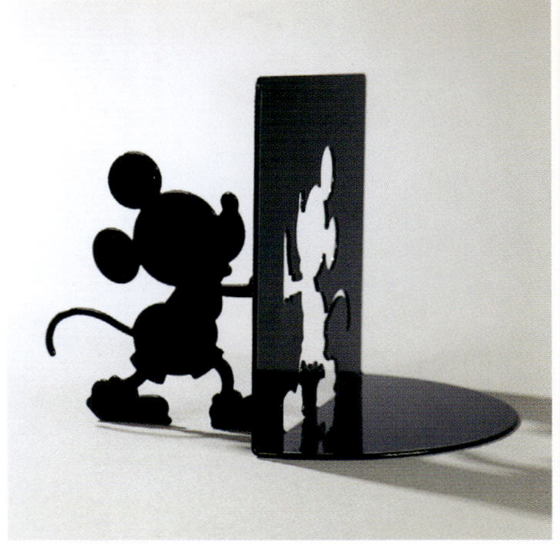

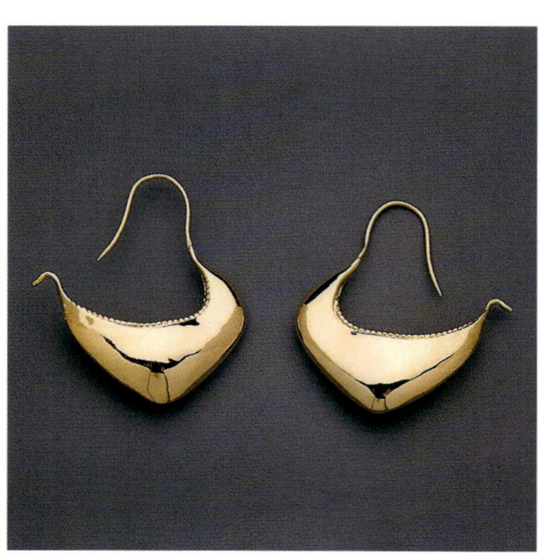

Clockwise from opposite top:

Dorsey chair produced by the David Edward Company, 1990

Kyoto chair for Arkitektura, 1989

Finestra chair for Atelier International, 1989

Custom dining room chair, 1989

Lounge chair produced by Design America, 1989

Sanders dining room chair, 1988

The open-number wall clock for Target (1999) evokes institutional clocks and signage of the Streamlined style.

Opposite top: Designers examining prototypes of mirrors for Target

Opposite bottom: In the studio's highly interactive work environment, product designers maintain constant dialogue about their work.

The Designing Life

In keeping with his self-description as a "general practitioner," Michael Graves himself maintains a hand in his firm's projects. On any given day, he may address design topics nonstop, from the proportions of an apartment tower in New York to the curve of a spoon. With a careful eye and an unerring pencil, he reviews designs at critical stages, suggesting improvements and focusing the creative process. At product design reviews, Graves wields a drawing pencil in one hand and in the other a roll of the see-through pale yellow tracing paper that is ubiquitous in architectural practices and called simply "trace." Graves likes to critique product designs in the form of AutoCAD drawings—simple elevations, like those of a blueprint. It makes the process objective, he feels.

Among other drawings, a dozen designs for a fondue set for Target confronted him one typical day. The basic designs were laid out at the bottom of the sheet in miniature silhouettes. Scanning them, he deployed bold and approving checkmarks here and decisive, even dismissive, X's there, over carefully worked out concepts that didn't make the grade.

The designers often visit the local Target store. They watch the weekly sales reports from Target like schoolboys tracking batting averages of their baseball heroes.

Graves numbered his five favorites in order of preference. Of them, only a couple would be chosen to be sampled and "value engineered" (a process that estimates how much they will cost to manufacture and how practical they are). To change a curve, he covered the drawing with a piece of tracing paper and redrew it. "This needs to be fuller, more of the ogee curve," Graves suggested, naming an S-shape used in architectural moldings, and ran the pencil over the shape of the dish. Sometimes he can't resist working directly on the drawing itself.

There was a shorthand to the process that reflected years of work together and the shared design language of the firm.

Although the firm has grown to include more than one hundred employees, its foundations have remained consistent over the years, based on the teaching philosophy that Graves developed in nearly forty years at Princeton University. Unlike many star architects whose teachings are based on the rigors of their own aesthetic preferences, Graves' approach encouraged students to find their own voices. His strong belief in the theory that architecture and design are like language extended from the classroom to his professional practice, where variations and transformations flourished in a creative design environment. In Graves' firm, there is no one aesthetic, rather a common language spoken in many voices.

Graves has worked with a core group of people—his six partners and numerous senior staff—for an average of twenty years. And every year, new talent arrives. The practice is organized as a series of design studios: four architecture studios, each led by one of Graves' partners (Gary Lapera, Patrick Burke, John Diebboll, and Tom Rowe), an interiors studio, and four product design studios. (The two other partners, Karen Nichols, also an architect, and Susan Howard, the CFO,

manage the practice and the business.) The studio heads are responsible for project design and implementation with Michael Graves as their mentor. While Graves himself is actively involved on the drafting boards, drawing alongside his colleagues and providing the overall design vision for the work, the practice he has built capitalizes on the design abilities of his partners and staff.

"One of the most important attributes of this firm," says partner Gary Lapera, "is that everyone contributes ideas." The studios, which refer to themselves as "teams," each take on a wide variety of projects, large and small, from creating a new model for a chain of sports and entertainment complexes from master plan to T-shirts, to finding an innovative way to use technology on exterior lighting and house numbers in products being designed for Target.

The product design group emerged from the architectural practice in the late 1980s as the number of purely product commissions grew and, in 2003, formally became the Michael Graves Design Group. However, the overall practice remained highly integrated. Interaction between architecture and product design gave the Graves firm a special perspective. In 2003, for instance, one of the architecture studios took the lead in designing products for Progress Lighting. The interiors department, sensing a market need for upholstered chairs, initiated a program that led to a new upholstered furniture collection for the David Edward Company. And the products studio jumped in to design dinnerware for restaurants that the architects were creating for luminary chefs Jean-Georges Vongerichten and David Laris in a new Shanghai arts and retail center.

"**This** place is not ego-driven," observes Donald Strum, senior director of product design. "Michael enjoys the team environment and interaction. He likes sharing knowledge and taking part in the back-and-forth." Designers have learned to internalize Graves' tastes and tendencies and sometimes reject their own initial drawings, noting that "we have to make it more 'Michael.'" Elements of the Graves design language are tagged the "Egyptian foot" or the "Giotto star," the five-sided ornamental device that stands in his universe for the celestial and ethereal. The Giotto star was inspired by the star in the frescoes of the great Paduan master of the early Renaissance. It can show up in the decorative pattern on a deck of cards in a board game or punched in stainless steel in the heating element of the fondue set.

In the hands of an MGDG modelmaker, the base of a proposed table lamp is sanded down.

Wooden dowels in a variety of sizes are kept on hand in the firm's modelmaking shop.

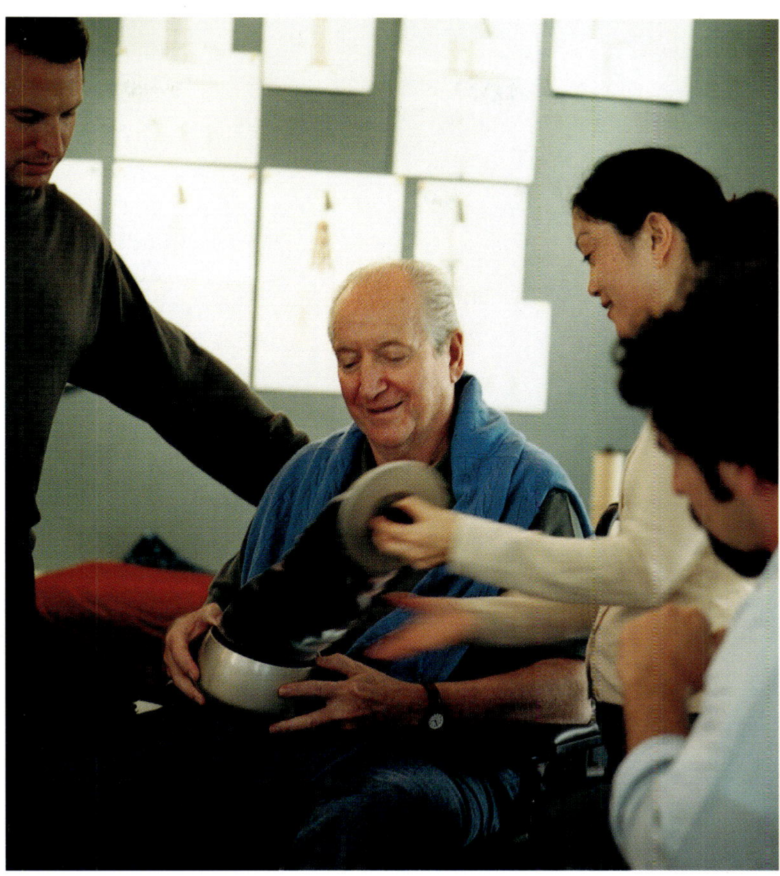

Top: Michael Graves scrutinizes product prototypes presented to him by the staff.

Above: The designers often sketch by hand in the earliest stages of a project, later using the computer to refine their designs.

Following pages: The Jackpot CD holder for Target, inspired by the Slinky, adds interest and functionality to a desktop.

The "house of cards" is a phrase that Graves uses to refer to intersecting planes—in the legs of kitchen stools, for instance. It brings to mind the classic game of intersecting cards designed by Charles and Ray Eames in 1952.

In his design reviews, the renditions Graves rejects are almost always those that are unclear or overly complex. He is always very insistent on the clarity and integrity of the basic form. He often resists younger designers' efforts to add different materials and colors that dilute the shape. "The ideal we have around here," Strum says, "is to create a form that a layperson can draw from memory."

At another review session, a group of designers were considering ideas for a future steam iron. They helped themselves to coffee, twisting open the top of a Graves-designed Target carafe, and gathered around a set of sketches. Graves had long admired the robust General Electric flatirons of the 1930s. In lectures, he showed one beside an image of a Streamlined locomotive from the era of Raymond Loewy. The locomotive dwarfed a man standing beside it; and, looking at the iron, it was easy to imagine a tiny toy figure next to it, as in one of Target's playful advertisements in which Graves' products are rendered larger than life,

Families

For the initial Target line, themes, such as Thebes and Tripod, were used to create "product families." The Thebes series of home accessories, clocks, and frames featured cut-out metal shapes. Tripod was a series of clocks, frames, and candleholders with a three-part "foot" or base inspired by an artifact from Pompeii.

The family of products idea had begun with Graves' work for Alessi. The teakettle for Alessi had been followed by accessories—mugs, creamer, salt and pepper shakers, espresso pot—of similar look and color, similar design "genes." One such gene was the pattern of rivets at the base of the teakettle. The design language of the Target products suggested a similar family relation: the coffee-bean grinder, for example, seemed to be the offspring of the toaster and blender. The Target themes were much less formal and more dynamic—and more American, perhaps—than those for Alessi.

Top: Tripod family for Target, 1999

Bottom: Thebes family for Target, 1999

“The family of products concept started with the idea that you touch most of the things in the kitchen,” Graves says. “When you pick up a spatula, you want to know you will touch a cool handle and that it will feel good. The shapes are not abstract, like modernist design objects, where you don’t know which end to pick up.”

For electronics, the keynote was simplicity and character. The black-and-white desk telephone seemed to have been plucked out of the past, but from an indeterminate era. The answering machine was simple; the cordless phone hung on the wall. The approach was a reaction against the proliferation of buttons and knobs that made such seemingly simple appliances as telephones to clock radios challenging to operate. Retailing tended to favor the addition of more buttons, more features, to outdo the competition. In the famous “blender wars” of the 1970s, rival makers put five, ten, even eighteen speeds on their machines, most of which were indistinguishable in effect from the next. By contrast, Graves understood that simplicity could itself become a competitive feature.

Top: Telephones and electronic products for Target, 1999–2000

Above: One of the “families” Graves created for Alessi in 1988–89 featured glass with gridded bands of stainless steel.

A wireless computer mouse for Target was inspired by the smooth, comfortable shapes of worn ocean rocks. Through successive models, the form became both organic and ergonomic.

Following pages: Meetings and design reviews occur both formally and informally in the new office space for the Michael Graves Design Group.

and tiny people interact with them in unexpected ways (such as rock-climbing the face of a cribbage board). Both shapes spoke of speed and efficiency. Graves liked the fact that on the Streamlined-style iron, a simple turn of the thumb controlled the temperature. The iron implied speeding through the dull task of ironing like an express train through the night.

The plumper, less sleek shapes under consideration spoke instead of "bouncing" through the job. They were more playful and cartoonish. One designer wanted to add a speed line to the shape, but Strum resisted. Such a line would dilute the impact of the overall shape, which, in any Graves design, represented its essence.

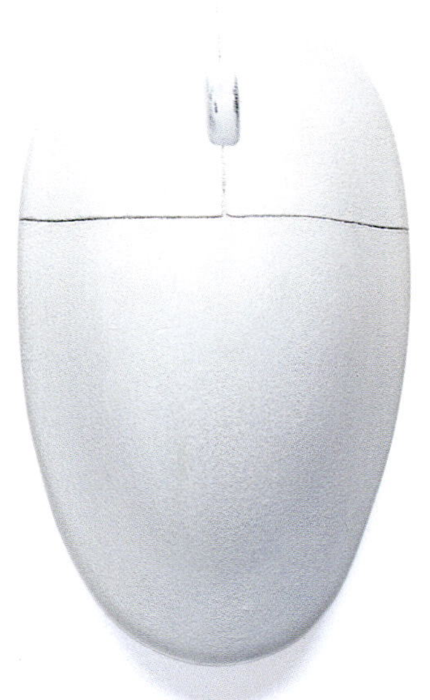
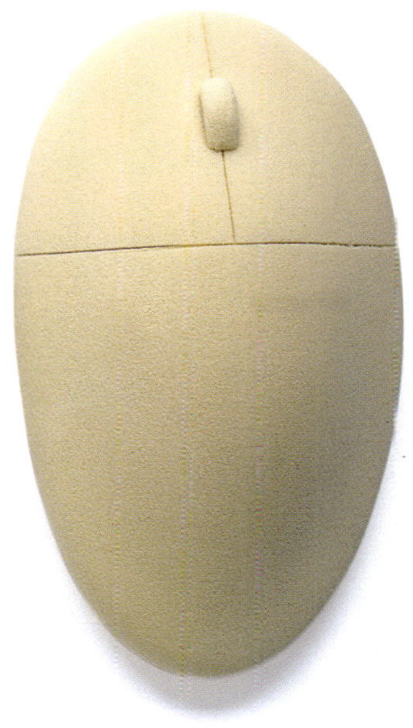

With the formal establishment of the Michael Graves Design Group in 2003, a third building near the same corner in Princeton was acquired and remodeled into additional product design offices. With large double-hung windows, the new space maintains the domestic feel of the other buildings, but its main workspace is large, sunny, and almost loftlike in its spaciousness—quite a contrast to the close quarters of the old houses, where the feeling had gone from cozy to cramped. "We were jammed in there shoulder to shoulder," said Linda Kinsey, senior director of product development. With several design teams decamped to the new office, everyone has gained more room.

The new building is wheelchair-accessible, and Graves, in addition to keeping his old office in the brick building, will now work there. In early 2003, while traveling on business, Graves was struck with an illness that has left him partially paralyzed. His hands and arms are, fortunately, unaffected, and he draws as well as ever.

Across long banks of desks and monitors in the studio, the new space is open to the exchange of ideas. One wall is lined with a generous expanse of fabric-covered tackboard for pinning up drawings. On another wall hang two Graves clocks of two different designs, side by side. One is marked Princeton. The other Minneapolis, home base of Target. It's a wry joke about the relationship with the retailer. While the two clocks are set only one hour apart, they remind the designers of the different senses of time in the two organizations.

The new office, of course, maintains the casual atmosphere of the others. Designers sometimes even bring their children or their dogs. On any given day, work in the offices is a quiet but steady buzz of design and conversation. Pens and computer mice in hand, the Graves staff generates ideas and sketches, but also deals with practical and human crises. Much of the work is collaborative, and so there are near-constant phone discussions, emails, faxes, and meetings. Staff members work with their team, clients, manufacturing plants, and vendors. Expected and unexpected conferences and problems arise.

News from a factory always requires immediate attention, as it could otherwise mean a delay in production. When Strum had an email from an Asian factory waiting for him one recent morning, alerting him that there was a problem with a new teakettle design for Target, it became his top priority for the morning. The factory managers said they could not make the kettle's conical spout, but since the firm has designed other kettles with conical spouts, Strum didn't understand the problem. A colleague soon clarified: The machines at the factory could make conical spouts, but the cones produced a higher ratio of defective products than a simpler cylindrical spout. Adding fifty cents to the price of the kettle would cover the waste and make the design work, and Strum agreed to approach Target about the extra cost.

Across the street, the firm's dedicated model-making shop buzzed. Scattered around were several half-finished models: an assemblage of wooden rectangles on a board making up a university campus and several unpainted kitchen tools in a pale tan porous material, like larval versions of the mature tools to come. Study models are made on-site of dense foam or wood and help the designers to get the shapes and proportions just right. As the design of a product proceeds, the models become more refined, in some cases requiring parts that cannot be made on-site. In those cases, Donald Menke, who runs the model shop, orders laser-cut acrylic parts from a company in California's Silicon Valley. The acrylic shapes become the templates for the control panels of new appliances and are integrated into a careful foam model he's made in Princeton. "At five o'clock, we can send a computer file by email with detailed information about a current product design," Menke explains. "The company uses the file to direct a laser to cut out the plate. They put it in overnight shipping by the end of their business day, and we get it the next morning." Cutting shapes with the laser is expensive, but it provides the precise templates some models require. Others are worked up by Menke directly on the lathe in his shop.

The designers often visit the local Target store. They watch the weekly sales reports from Target like schoolboys tracking the batting averages of their baseball heroes. They want to know how their designs are selling. Eric Bogner, head of one of the product design studios, stopped in at lunch recently and inspected the display of products. He noted with some dismay that a teakettle had been exiled to the bottom shelf in the housewares section—and there was no display model. He checked to see if the Graves toaster was also on display in the generic toaster area two rows over, whether it was "double-faced" (stocked in two aisles), and was happy to find it so: more shelf exposure means more sales. Because Bogner was leaving to visit a factory in Thailand the next day, he bought the remaining inventory of Graves bottle openers—a half dozen—to give out as gifts on his trip.

In addition to the periodic design critiques with Graves, the design staff meets weekly to update each other on the progress of projects and relations with various clients. In the conference room, surrounded by examples of past work, prototypes, and models, two dozen designers squeeze in to overflowing. Drawings and models and samples are shown. The meeting reveals the number and variety of projects that the office handles at any one time.

One day last fall, new rug samples for Glen Eden and a box of watches from Switzerland were on view. Everyone clustered around for a look. The meeting always begins with a show-and-tell—staff members offer ideas and images that intrigue and inspire them. That day, two new books, one on Russel and Mary Wright, another on Eva Zeisel, were presented by a young staffer.

From left:
Designers in Eric Bogner's studio review prototypes and models for wall mirrors, stemware, and more.

Judy Gawlowski oversees the details of Graves' packaging for Target.

Dodie Colavecchio sands a model of a proposed product for Dansk.

Designers make notes of changes to prototypes which are delivered, examined, and returned to the factories often within a single day.

Since individual designers deal with various buyers at Target—at least five different Target departments are involved—and numerous other clients, there are always several reports to be made. A young woman named Yuka Midorikawa held up gleaming Rhino drawings of salad and serving pieces for Dansk, aimed at department store sales. These took a theme of "Scandinavian on a slant"—a new twist on the Danish modern for which the company's dishes, casseroles, and other items were known in the past. A martini shaker for Target had a clever "olive" shape as its stopper. "The original idea was a kind of black rubber ball, like a Superball," Midorikawa reported. "The client wants it green now." The group acknowledged that this associative touch was a good idea.

There was an ice bucket and glasses—simple shapes, set off by a slanting upper surface, a slice off the top that gives them a bit of attitude. "Are these giftable?" quipped a retail-savvy designer. Going along with the inside joke, Midorikawa responded, "Very giftable."

Word came that a new line of garden furniture for another client had been put on hold. "We know what that means," Strum observed philosophically. The line would almost surely die.

The number of ideas and designs that will ever see production is only a tiny fraction of those generated. Changes in clients and buyer tastes doom many. In a single day, a number are proven impractical for reasons of material, cost, or fabrication. The staff must leave the casualties behind and move on. Offering a prescription for happiness for designers, Bogner says, "You have to enjoy the process, not the product." ■

Michael Graves on **Color**

For me, color—along with form—is representational. The colors that I use in my buildings often refer to natural construction materials or to the landscape itself. To root a building on its site, I tend to use heavier colors at the base, colors that are suggestive of the landscape, such as terracotta or other earthen tones, as well as green. As the building rises toward the sky, the colors tend to get lighter, more ephemeral. They don't have to be literally sky blue, of course, and it's possible to invert the emphasis top to bottom, so long as the choices are not arbitrary. For example, a building along a river or the interior of a spa might use blue and white or even golden tiles to represent the flicker of light on water. A trellis supporting climbing vines above a window or a porch made of wood might be colored differently from the masonry body of the building to correspond with its different use, materials, and scale. ◆ As with form in a figurative approach to design, color has a language and thus can be used to convey meaning. It can represent another entity in an abstracted way, and it can also be used to differentiate the formal parts of a building or a product. For example, the spherical Big Dripper coffeepot designed

Left: Sheraton Miramar Hotel on the Red Sea in El Gouna, Egypt, 1995

Right: Health club pools at the El Gouna Golf Hotel and Club, 1997

Bottom: Nylon whisk with Santoprene handle for Target, 2000

for Swid Powell has a cruciform base in a dark reddish terra-cotta color; the color connotes ground and, in this case, also heat. Above that, on the body of the pot, wavy green lines suggest water. In our Alessi teakettle, the handle is blue, implying coolness to the touch, and the bird on the spout where the steam emerges is red, indicating heat. I had wanted to make the round dots at the base of the kettle red also, because of their proximity to the flame of the stove, but that was technically not feasible. The products we've designed for Target follow this same color logic and as the families of, say, countertop appliances and kitchen tools grow, consistent use of color creates identity for those collections and a cohesive presence in the kitchen.

The completed scaffold for the Washington Monument, seen at night, was a critical and popular success.

A Familiar and Fascinating Landmark

Graves saw in the scaffolding an opportunity to create a temporary yet highly visible work that would speak to a diverse public on many levels.

Today, no one can quite remember who first mentioned Michael Graves' name, but many recall that Target executives wanted a designer "with wit." The job description called for creating a special scaffolding to cover the Washington Monument, the 555-foot-high obelisk dedicated to the nation's first president and inspired by ancient Egypt by way of Rome. The renovation would last two full years, a brief footnote for a structure more than a century old—yet long enough to demand special consideration. Government officials did not want a crude construction site towering over the National Mall in plain view of the White House, and had asked the Minneapolis-based retailer Target Stores for help in sponsoring an outside-the-box solution.

Target approached Graves in 1997, opening the first chapter in a fruitful association. Along with his drafting tools, Graves brought to the table much more than just wit. He was, at the time, working on a government building, the Ministry of Health and Sport in The Hague, and had been thinking about the role of architecture in fostering civic spirit. The same interest had animated the design of one of his earliest, most

Left: In an early design, the scaffolding was designed in wood, which quickly proved impractical.

Below: Graves first envisioned scaffolding for the monument inspired by Renaissance forms, conveyed in a 1596 etching by Domenico Fontana.

famous works, the public services building in Portland, Oregon. There, Graves had tried to create a symbol of government and history that was at once accessible and imposing. Monuments to great leaders were the purest form of such imagery. He saw in the scaffolding an opportunity to create a temporary yet highly visible work that would speak to a diverse public on many levels. The project, as Graves imagined it, riffed on many of his favorite themes: populism, Americana, patriotism, tradition, and the ability of architecture to tell stories. He wanted the scaffolding to bring the obelisk's million annual visitors into a more intimate relationship with its history—and, by extension, the nation's.

Graves perceived that, thanks to its very familiarity, the Washington Monument had in some ways started to be taken for granted, to become invisible in plain sight. He set out to make it fascinating again. By hiding it he hoped paradoxically to reveal it and, as he says, "amplify" the process of restoration. The blue mesh sheath Graves created was a tour de force—a crowd-pleasing spectacle, part civic architecture and part pop art. The scaffolding had to make up, in effect, for the absence of the monument. The public would not be allowed to ride to the top of monument during renovation, and Graves wanted to compensate visitors for this loss with a sense of participating in the renovation. The scaffold drew rave reviews from such observers as *Washington Post* architecture critic Benjamin Forgey, *The NewsHour with Jim Lehrer,* and *Time* magazine. Its run, originally scheduled to end in late 1999, was held over into the following year to make it the focal point for the millennium fireworks display. Civic groups in Richmond, Virginia, and Minneapolis, Minnesota, explored moving the scaffolding and rebuilding it as a kind of "shadow" monument (an enterprise that ultimately proved impractical but confirmed the project's popularity).

"The goal was to tell a story about restoration," Graves says, "about monuments in general, obelisks, George Washington, that monument on the Mall, the axis of the capital, and so on."

Graves wanted to use the scaffolding to point to the past but also to a future where both the lessons and the monument—viewed as a potential terror target as early as 1998—would endure. He also wanted to make it clear that buildings need maintenance. "Buildings need health care the way people do," Graves says. With a shorter history than

The final scaffolding was constructed of conventional aluminum tubing, but the fabric was added in strips that mimicked the "running bond" pattern of the masonry itself.

Below: Commemorative painting by Michael Graves, 1998

Europeans, Americans were always quicker to cut a ribbon on a new building than to restore an old one. The scaffold could teach the lesson that public buildings need maintenance and refurbishment not only in a physical sense but also a spiritual one. Not only must the stones of monuments be cleaned and their joints repointed (the Washington Monument job involved cleaning and replacing mortar and expanding the interior to accommodate growing crowds), but their histories must be retaught and their meanings updated.

In Europe, older buildings are constantly under restoration. In fact, the combination of obelisk and scaffolding immediately reminded Graves of a church in Rome that was covered by scaffolding for the two years he lived in that city during the early 1960s. "When I returned twenty years later, it was still under scaffolding." He also thought of the once-famous scaffolding Domenico Fontana used in moving an obelisk into the middle of St. Peter's Square in 1596. That project, commemorated in a book issued by the Vatican, was one of the engineering wonders of the Renaissance. (Graves' collection of antique drawings includes Fontana's etching.)

Graves' first idea was to build a vast wooden scaffold like Fontana's, which quickly proved impractical due to the amount of lumber it would require—after all, it is the National Park Service that oversees the Washington Monument. Then he and Tom Rowe, the firm's principal in charge of the project, struck on the idea of a fabric screen that would both shield and amplify. As executed, the scaffold became a structure in itself, a cover for the monument sixteen feet wider than the original that dropped over it like a giant cake cover. Unlike standard scaffolding, it exactly replicated the tapered profile of the building. The skeleton required thirty-six miles of aluminum tubing, to which open-weave blue polyester fabric mesh was attached in the same pattern as the stones beneath—known to masons as "running bond." Workers could be seen through the mesh, revealing in Graves' mind two monuments: the one being worked on and its representation in the form of scaffolding.

Graves and Target undertook a subsequent project, which opened some months later, to renovate the interiors of the Monument at the observation level (500 feet above ground) and the interpretive level (490 feet), along with the cab of the public elevator that would

take visitors to those levels. Inside, exhibitions designed by Graves' office and a Richmond, Virginia–based design firm called 1717 Design Group highlighted the history and meaning of the obelisk, enriching the visitors' experience. Graves, who had taught architecture at Princeton and lectured widely for nearly forty years, now interpreted American history, world history, engineering, and construction for his largest audience yet.

The Washington Monument lies at the center of Pierre L'Enfant's original plan for Washington, D.C. Located on the Mall at the intersection of the axis between the Capitol and the Lincoln Memorial and the axis of the White House and the Jefferson Memorial, the Washington Monument was first planned as an equestrian statue. A later scheme, by noted architect Robert Mills, involved a colonnade surrounding a flat-topped obelisk. The tensions preceding the Civil War and the war itself interrupted construction, which resumed in 1876 under Lt. Col. Thomas L. Casey of the Army Corps of Engineers. Casey simplified Mill's design to what stands today, removing all hints of ornament. He modified the monument's proportions to match the Egyptian obelisk with a pyramidal cap that had been later adopted by the Romans. But, in keeping with the American love of size, the obelisk of the Washington Monument was built ten times larger than its Egyptian predecessors.

Construction was finished in 1884, and the obelisk was topped with aluminum, which was rare at the time. On the monument, the world's tallest structure until the Eiffel Tower came along in 1889, the line between the stone of the original and that of the resumed construction—the visible effects of twenty years' additional weathering—is clear to the visitor today.

The scaffold ultimately allowed tourists who visited during the renovation to still see and appreciate the iconic national treasure. Even for people who lived in the area and saw the monument regularly, Graves' design prompted a fresh appreciation. For Graves, the scaffolding had another consequence. Although it was, to date, his most public project, it led to much smaller, more private items—for the table and countertop—that would have an even wider popular impact. ■

Flyswatter for Target, 2002

Changing the World: Michael Graves Meets Target

By teaming with Target, Graves has achieved a goal that has eluded other designers for almost a century: bringing good design to a wide public.

While working with Target on the scaffolding for the Washington Monument in 1997, Michael Graves met various executives at Target, including senior merchants for home decor. Since they all agreed on the importance of design at affordable prices, Target asked if Graves would consider designing products for it to sell. Graves remembers them saying, "We've been following your work for years, so why not go right to the source?"

Graves had been seeking just such an alliance. "Ever since I was a student in Italy," he says, "I was struck by how Europeans valued good design differently from Americans. It became my goal to up the ante in the United States, to be able to offer well-designed objects to the public at reasonable prices. The majority of the early invitations I received to design objects came from established manufacturers with higher ranges of prices, but I made a determined decision to pursue manufacturers and distributors that could achieve design quality and yet come to market at affordable prices."

The launch of the Graves line of Target products was accompanied by advertising in the same original, witty, pop spirit: a billboard teakettle with real steam and toasters as big as buses.

Together, Target merchants and Graves visited a Target store, where the executives asked for his advice. Graves offered to walk through the store and put Post-it notes on all the products whose design he thought he could improve. One Target executive joked that there might not be enough Post-its.

Graves did not know Target well, but the more he learned, the more impressed he was. "It started very slowly," he recalls. "I never thought we would end up doing so many products." Small things about the company delighted him—for instance, that Target had posted ads on baseball outfield walls using their familiar bull's-eye logo as a home-run target for batters, evoking the "hit here, win a suit" teases on outfield walls of the 1950s.

Graves and his designers had previously worked primarily with manufacturers and distributors and had much to learn about how a retailer like Target does business. Timing is everything, beginning with the date on which a product arrives, or "sets," on the shelf. Plans to design and manufacture a product start with that date and work backward. Once displayed, a product, according to a retailing rule of thumb, has just eight seconds to capture the attention of a shopper, or in Target's parlance, a "guest."

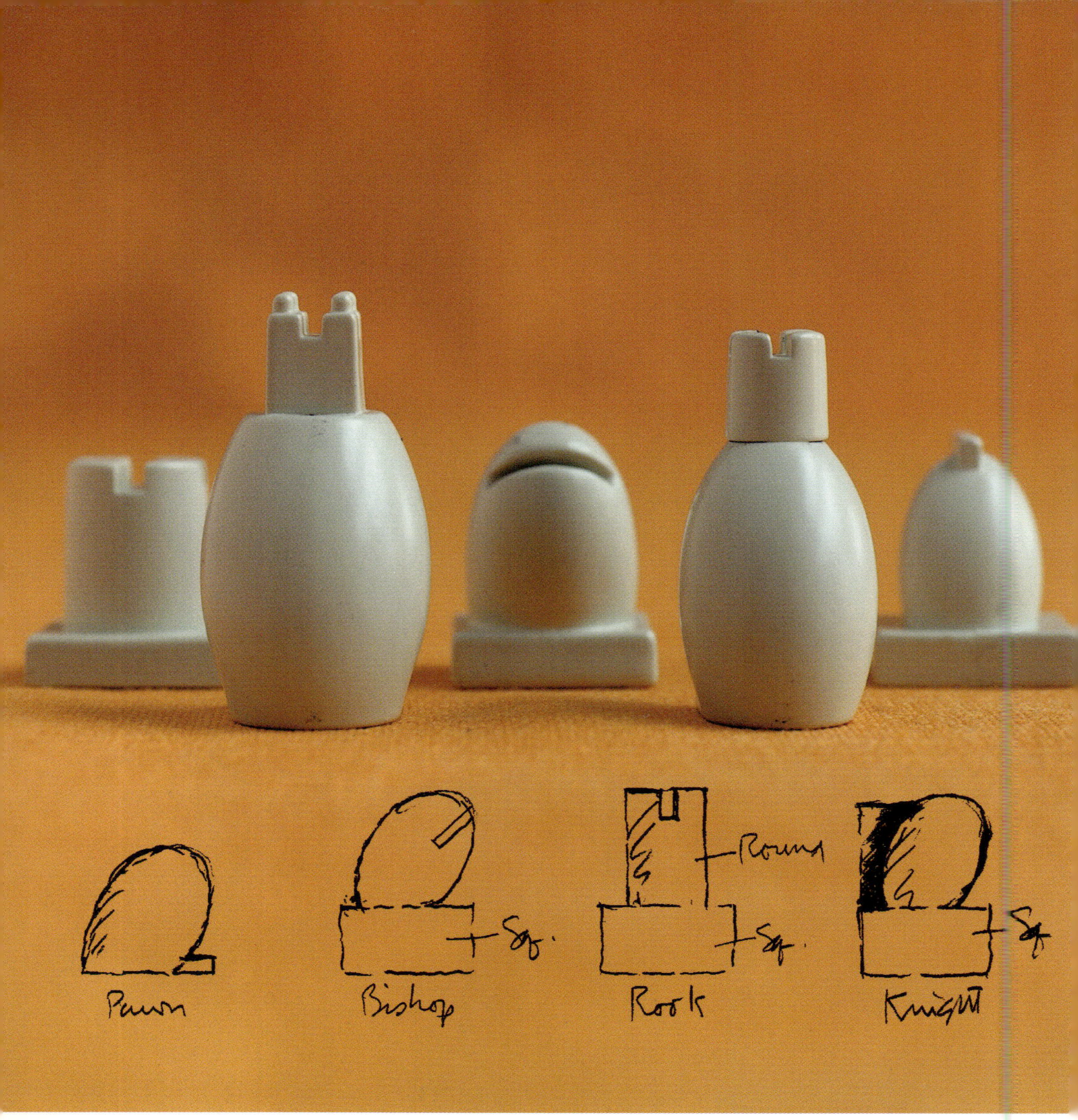

Products can succeed or fail in a matter of weeks, or even days. A product's shelf life is like the run of a film or play: buyers and store executives, when they place orders, are speculating on the potential success of any product. Too few units on hand and sales can be lost on popular products; too many and products that don't strike the fancy of guests languish until they are marked down or moved out. Products must evolve with time. Target depends on repeat customers and, like other retailers, is tied to seasonal rhythms: back-to-school, holidays, and so on. "Target kept reminding us that two years is a lifetime in this business," says Linda Kinsey, senior director of product development. Graves understood that his firm would be working not just with the Target buying team—as in the department store tradition, they were key decision makers—but also with the many suppliers and their factories all over the world.

The arrival of the so-called big-box stores, which began to cluster along American highways in the 1990s like ships at anchor, selling discount building supplies, electronics, office equipment, and general merchandise, had changed American retailing. These mega-discount stores were changing the country's shopping sensibility at the same time that chains like Banana Republic, Pottery Barn, and Williams-Sonoma were spreading the idea of well-designed goods at reasonable prices across the country.

At a time when finding bargains had become chic, Target's audience was growing, especially among young women who pronounced it in mock French as "tar-zhay." Target's bull's-eye became one of the country's best-known logos, and the company's witty print and television ads became familiar—including small newspaper ads with figures clambering over objects, which played on visual puns and scale tricks.

Target was founded in 1962—the same year as Kmart. But while Kmart grew out of the five-and-dime, Target was the offspring of a classic Midwestern department store, Dayton Hudson, with a tradition of giving customers value and style, not just low prices. As in deparment stores, critical power at Target lies in the hands of the buyers, who know their departments, their guests, and the products in their categories. Target also carried from the department store the idea of merchandising as theater—as at Neiman Marcus, with its outrageous, attention-grabbing special products, such as his-

When Target gave Graves the chance to redesign traditional board games, he immediately thought of the legacy of architect-designed chess sets from the Bauhaus of the 1920s.

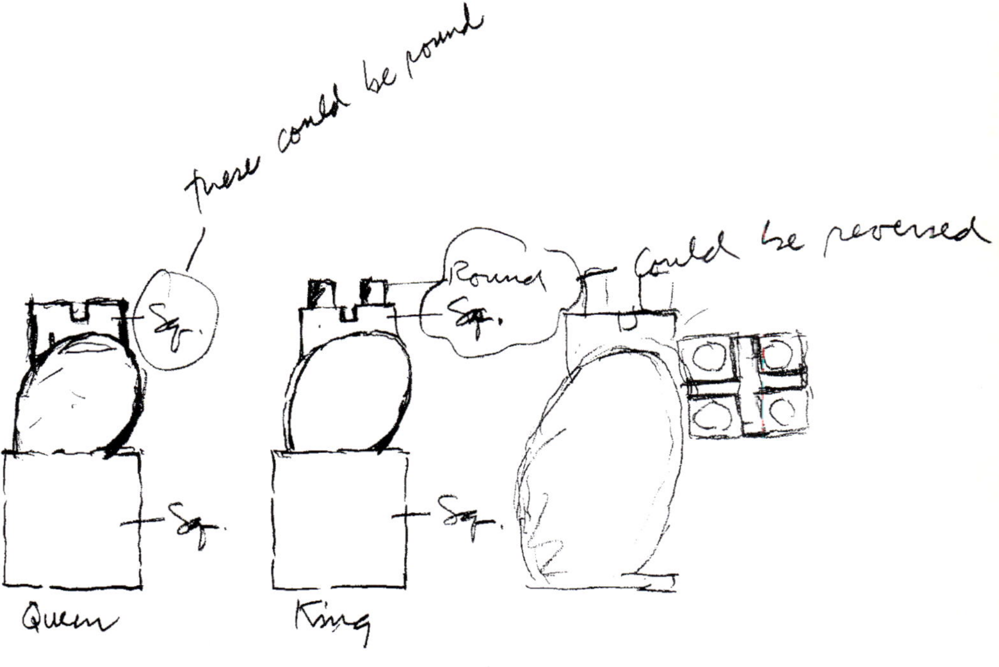

and-her private planes, or Bloomingdale's, with its rotating themed presentations of, say, Italian products throughout its stores.

Graves and Target agreed to work together. By December 1997, a troop of Target executives visited Graves' office in Princeton. The fact that Graves had his own store—tiny as it was—impressed Target. It gave them confidence that he would be aware of the realities of retailing, of inventory, and of merchandising.

During the first round of meetings, it was agreed that Graves would devise a whole range of products. The collection would include kitchen gadgets and countertop appliances, garden furniture and clocks, frames and candleholders.

Graves and his staff learned that in retail-speak a "run" was a four-foot range of shelving. Six runs made up one gondola, which terminated in two "end caps," each an area for display of products as well. The Graves kitchen items eventually got their own gondola, complete with Graves' signature and logo cut into metal, swelling like a bay window above the shelves. But other items would be scattered around the store in appropriate categories.

Top: Graves creates architectural diagrams of products on Target shelves that closely resemble the fully stocked shelves.

Above: Ice bucket for Target, 1999

This presentation was a balanced solution. In such a vast environment, Graves' studio saw the benefits of gathering their products into dense groupings. Target, on the other hand, did not want to create a Graves boutique, but to shelve the products throughout the store to surprise and delight the guest. A Graves mop might be displayed beside a can of floor wax. "Target wanted a halo factor," says Linda Kinsey. "They wanted to have the store studded with Graves products."

Graves was hired not for his name but for his design. Indeed, Target's early surveys showed that only about 25 percent of store visitors had heard of him. On visits to Target stores, in both informal and formal appearances, Graves found that he was only occasionally recognized—more often by children than adults. His picture and a brief bio were printed on the boxes, but for those who did not take time to read the packaging, Graves might become a symbol for design itself. Some shoppers wondered whether Michael Graves might even be an invented figure, like Betty Crocker. Patrick Burke, an architect and principal of Graves' firm, visited a Target store not long after the collection appeared and got into a discussion with a customer. "Michael Graves designs buildings, too?" the woman asked.

The designs grabbed center stage. Target executives have said, "Some stores are price-driven. We wanted to be idea-driven. Our guests can connect with an idea more readily than an item." Target was selling emotions and visions of lifestyle, rather than simply individual goods. It was exactly the same sentiment often expressed by Murray Moss, the retailer known for his luxury design shop in SoHo in New York. Moss, respected as a careful connoisseur of the best in international design, told *Graphis* magazine, "I am selling not things but ideas."

Target's products, some shipped directly from factory to shelves, must sell quickly or be discounted. One of the company's key slogans, "Speed is life," embodies the old retailing precept of rapid turnover. Available for a limited time and rarely reordered, the products could, in effect, turn into collectibles. Ironically, the more popular a product is, the faster it will sell and the shorter its life on the shelf. When the Graves products appeared, observers understood their collectability. Reed Kroloff wrote in *Architecture* magazine, "The aim is to create collectibles for the common man." Around the Graves office, the saying was, "Design lasts, retail does not."

Many Target shoppers testify—to the delight of store executives—that they go in the store looking for one thing and come out with a handful of items they never planned to buy. Because the store faces tough competition from other discount retailers on price, it was vital that

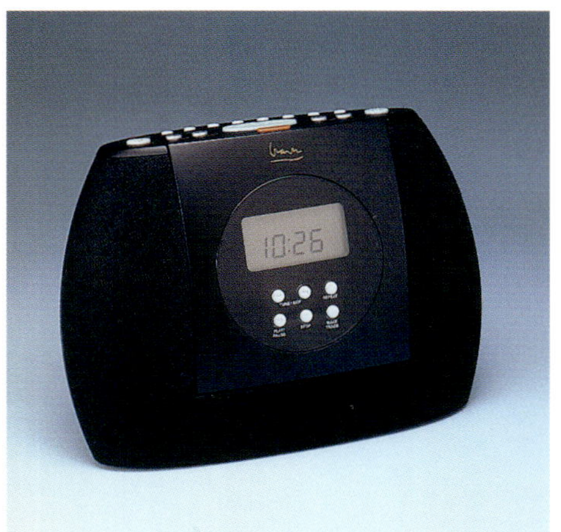

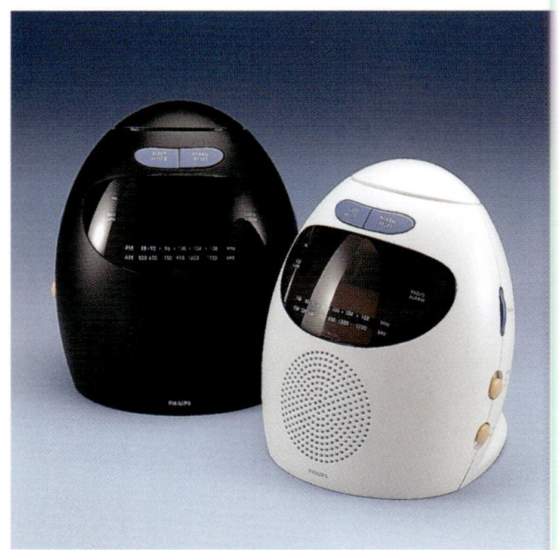

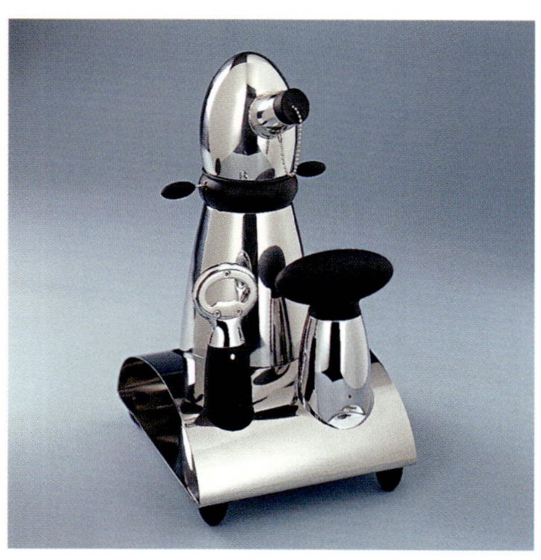

Swivel alarm clock, 2003

CD clock radio, 2002

Rachel task lamp, 2001

Barware set, 2002

Glass clock, 2003

Egg clock radios, 2000

Ceramic pitcher, 2003

Table fan, 2001

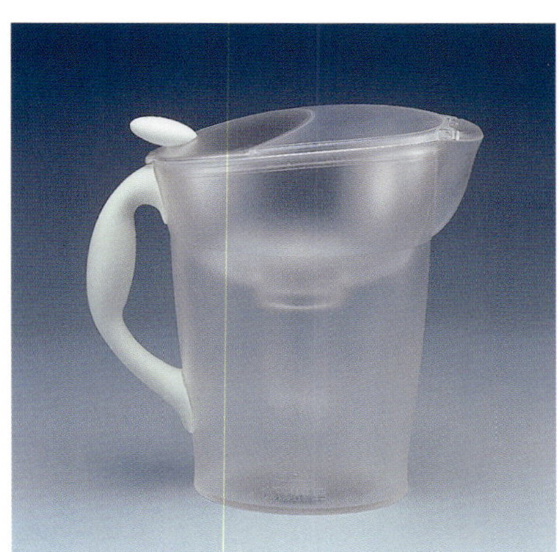

Cutting board and knife, 2003

Chess set, 2000

Brita® water pitcher, 2003

Fondue set, 2002

Bathroom scale, 2003

Knife block and knives, 2003

Thermal carafe, 2001

Bent plywood magazine rack, 2003

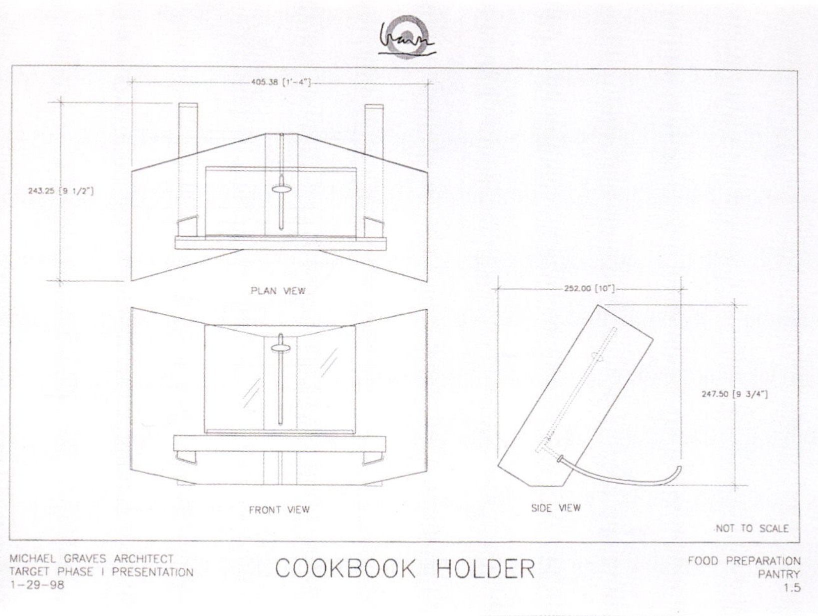

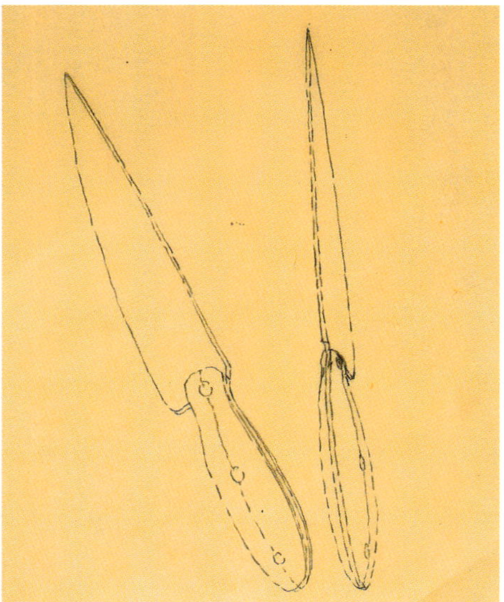

The first product design drawings presented to Target were too technical to be accessible, so Graves started making three-dimensional drawings that more easily represented what the products would look like.

Target offer unique products—what management calls "non-redundant" products. Target had already moved to secure key brands (Bodum and Calphalon kitchen products and Philips electronics, among others) and presented some items in colors not sold at other stores. Target liked exclusive merchandise. It alone launched Sony's LIV series of clock radios and shower CD players aimed primarily at women, one design of which, the radio shaped like a woman's handbag, is a phenomenal hit. Target is the exclusive seller of another line of personal electronics, for Virgin, launched in 2003.

Once Graves and Target agreed to the collaboration, things moved swiftly. The Graves team had one month to produce a list of designs for the approximately two hundred products that they would pitch for the initial launch, four months to complete the designs, and only a year to deliver finished products to the stores. It was almost overwhelming. Linda Kinsey found herself in charge of executing this new venture with only five dedicated people to start with, though the staff rapidly grew to reflect the workload. The Graves staff later joked, "We lived the motto—speed was our life!"

In January 1998 Target buyers and executives arrived in Princeton to look at the first crop of designs, and the Graves office presented a comprehensive book of fairly technical line drawings. "We showed the drawings and there was silence," recalls Donald Strum, Graves' senior director of product design. "They couldn'tread them. They were not accustomed to being clients in a design process. Two-dimensional drawings didn't give them enough information." The Target team needed to see three-dimensional versions of the products. As the front-line soldiers of the company's marketing efforts, they needed to know how things, preferably finished products, would look on the shelves of a typical Target store.

Graves and his designers quickly understood that they had to produce clearer images of their ideas. For the next round, and all rounds since, they worked up three-dimensional renderings as well as painted models.

As part of this visualization and planning process, every season Michael Graves Design Group collaborates with Target on planograms—diagrams that map out the product assortment and merchandising strategy. In others' hands, planograms are simple black-and-white line drawings, but Graves takes that process one step further to document in an architectural fashion just what the shelf layout will look like. He says he uses it as "a canvas for painting a picture."

The impact products made on the shelves was better expressed in models, as of the best-selling toilet brush (2000).

Metal toilet brush for Target, 2002

In January 1999 the Target products were launched with a party at the Whitney Museum of American Art in New York, complete with a "clock of clocks," a pop-art assemblage of teakettles, and chandeliers composed of kitchen tools.

The kickoff for the new line came on January 19, 1999, with a party at the Whitney Museum of American Art in New York. The Graves staff, Target representatives, and a graphic design firm called Design Guys from Minneapolis completely redecorated the public spaces of the museum for the party—in one day. They built a chandelier from the Target kitchen tools, placed dozens of teakettles on one wall of the museum, and created a giant clock made of Target clocks. (The clocks were all set at ten minutes after ten—Graves' formula for making them smile.) Vases from the collection were filled with tulips and sat like works of art on cantilevered shelves. Graves, who understood the need for a bit of theater in retailing, even designed a special label for the wine bottles.

The party at the Whitney drew major press coverage. Graves did many interviews and appeared in Target stores. In the ad campaign that followed, Graves declared a determination to bring good design "to the everyday things we all need," promising "never to give up function for design" and to prove "that good design doesn't have to be so serious or so seriously expensive." Other ads had clever slogans—such as "the hipper flipper" (for the spatula) and "toast modern"—that

The Egg

Top: The egg shape is used both two- and three-dimensionally and abstracted in such designs as a 1930s-inspired kitchen wall clock for Target, 1999.

Above: The versatile egg shape surfaced in Graves' product designs for Alessi, for example, in the handle for an early 1990s model for a proposed espresso pot. The egg was eliminated from the pot's final design, but reappeared in other products.

The theme of the first Target collection, a whimsical shape that would link its different elements in form and character, was the egg. "I had just read a survey of architects and designers," Graves recalled later. "There was a consensus that the most beautiful shape was the egg."

The egg shape had surfaced before in Graves' work. For the glass manufacturer Glaskoch Leonardo, Graves had designed an aptly egg-shaped glass egg cup and a matching glass teakettle with an egg-shaped handle and an egg-shaped tea infuser. Also in the set was a glass teacup whose handle was a drooped egg shape.

The egg also appeared on the handle of one alternative design for the Alessi espresso pot, eventually called the Pelicano. "Alberto Alessi didn't like it," Graves recalls. "He said it wasn't 'pottish' enough." Graves has a way of never forgetting a good idea, though, and resurrected the egg for Target. Feet and knobs, handles and controls all took on versions of the oval and egg shape. The lid of the Target teakettle and the top of the electric coffeemaker were yellow, angled, egglike shapes.

The curves of the egg were echoed in the bodies of the toaster and other small appliances and in the quarter-moon arc of the knife block. Similar curves showed up in handles and buttons that were almost toylike, playfully large and swelling, welcoming the user's touch. There were an egg-shaped clock radio and a CD player.

For the clock radio the egg was enlarged to cantaloupe size so that it also suggested an astronaut's helmet. The egg was turned into a container for the headphones of the Target portable CD player. Like a child's coin purse, it was slit up the side to accommodate the earphones.

The egg was central to a series of glass objects designed for the German company Glaskoch Leonardo in 1996–98, including a teacup with an egg-shaped handle (never produced), the Nanna teakettle (with clever "well winch" mechanism for the steeper), and an elegant cup named Angel for the egg itself.

Below: For Target, the egg has often been set at a jaunty angle in handles and controls, as in the coffee bean grinder, 2001.

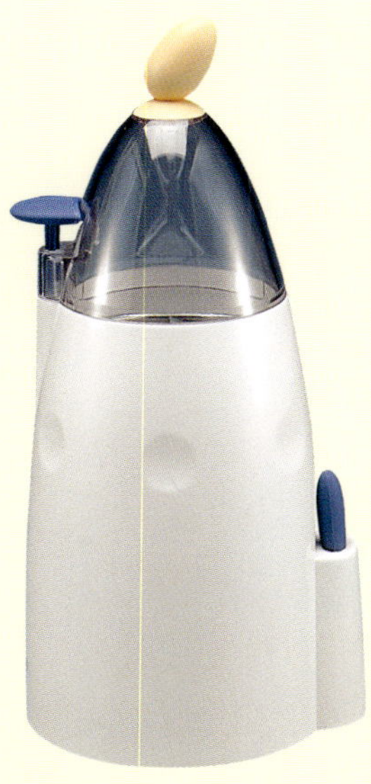

Common office objects—such as a paper shredder (2002)—are made more useful in Graves' hands by the addition of a pencil sharpener to the top.

meshed perfectly with the lighthearted wit of the products themselves. In Minneapolis a billboard for the teakettle was designed with steam coming out of the spout.

Customers and the media alike compared the Target products to those for Alessi and other clients. Where the Alessi teakettle had sold briskly at $125, the Target iteration was $25. "There are naturally constraints to working for a discounter," Graves says, "but I'm as proud of these objects as of anything I've ever done. Everything has a budget. In architecture, it's the difference between stucco and marble. In products, it's maybe plastic instead of porcelain or glass. Or you can do a candy dish in silver for Tiffany and one in aluminum for Target. The design energy remains the same."

One of the best-sellers among the Graves products was the toilet brush—making the most humble of products into a star. Virginia Postrel focused on it in her book, *The Substance of Style,* about the effect of design on what we buy. Postrel marveled at the variety of designer toilet brushes available, from one by Philippe Starck to Alessi's dolphin models to expensive gold and silver varieties. None sells as well as the Graves model for Target.

To John Pellegrene, Target's retired executive vice president of marketing, nothing better proved Graves' genius. "That he could take something as mundane as a toilet brush and turn it into a best-seller is amazing. Graves' great genius is that he can make even really everyday things look great," he says.

The dialogue between Target and Graves continues, and, like a true conversation, it goes both ways. Target believed in the value of spotting seasonal trends in colors and materials. Graves' people were leery. They didn't believe fashions either changed so fast or mattered so much, and, as Graves puts it, "We wanted to set the trends, not follow them." But in time Graves bought into Target's desire to create something new and exciting for the guests.

Graves also acknowledges that Target was right, for instance, in thinking that a paper shredder would become a big seller. Graves had been skeptical. Target insisted. In the Princeton Target store, frequented by Graves and his staff, the shredder was displayed in the office products aisle, far from any other Graves products and opposite the house plants. Released in April 2003, shortly before tax day and at a time when news coverage of identity theft was running high, it sold thousands within a few days. The Graves shredder had two advantages—one functional and one aesthetic—over its competition. It cleverly included an electric pencil sharpener on top, and its sleek shape and dignified black-and-silver color scheme made it more attractive than its strictly utilitarian counterparts. "I was surprised that the paper shredder did well," Graves says. "It didn't seem to me to be in the right place. But the first week we sold several thousand. And even at Target one thousand can be a home run."

Graves and his designers produced powerful and sensuous forms that could give a pepper mill (1999), an oil sprayer (2001), timer (1999), and a corkscrew (2002) dramatic presence in the kitchen.

Target's advertising charmed the stores' fans with witty taglines and plays on scale: a feather duster became a palm tree and a cribbage board, a rock climbing wall.

target.com
michael graves design™ expandable trivet $8.99 For store info. call 1.800.800.8800

achieve lift

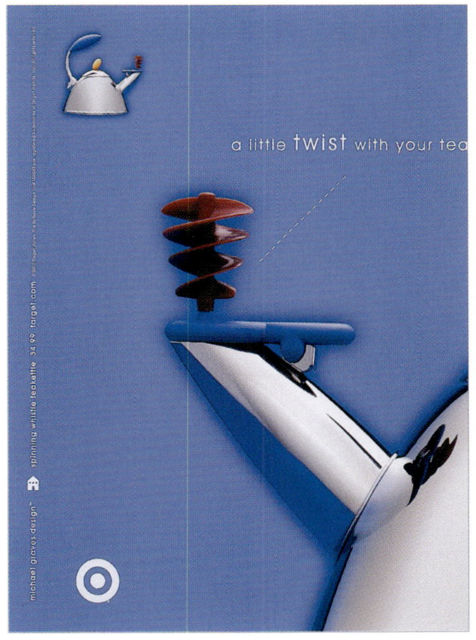
a little twist with your

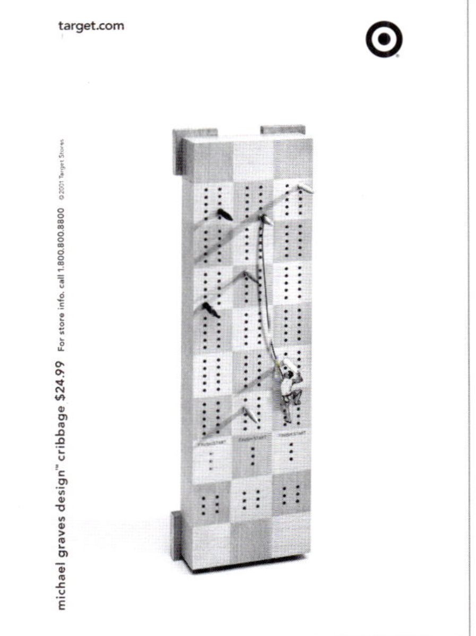
target.com
michael graves design™ cribbage $24.99 For store info. call 1.800.800.8800

It was Graves who suggested redesigning classic board games, believing that a redesign could breathe new life into them. He began with chess and checkers and then broadened out with Monopoly, Stratego, Scrabble, and dominoes. Graves had long thought he could improve upon the chess set designed by Josef Hartwig at the Bauhaus, having always considered the pieces too abstract. And he says, "I had always wanted to create a chess set." Graves sculpted the pieces like black-and-white eggs at a combative angle, but with powerful personalities transmitted by the simplest of curves and with ranks signaled by vestigial headgear. The pieces' abstract shapes suggest the directions the pieces move. "I like to take the bishops with the little slit on the top and use them at dinner parties as place-card holders," Graves says. For Monopoly, he designed a deluxe board in cherry that could be displayed proudly on a family room shelf between books. A built-in velvet-lined drawer holds the playing pieces, which he redesigned as miniature silver models of his Target products. Instead of the shoe, the iron, and the top hat, there is the toaster, the telephone, and the teakettle. He rendered the houses (in Graves Blue, of course) as the Graves logo that appears on Target packaging. And the hotel—in red—is reminiscent of the government ministry tower he designed in The Hague.

The Graves-Target relationship is ambitious. The ordinary citizen in the aisles of Target, the clerk who stocks the shelves, even the manager might not notice it, but the words on the blue Graves boxes express profound goals. Written collaboratively by Target and Graves, they declare a desire to merge the "simple and the sublime," "the practical and the poetic," or the warm and the whimsical"—hardly the standard retail pitch for kitchen spatulas or dustpans. Such language stands out, though, on retail shelves more accustomed to such clichés as "new and improved." For a retailer to declare its goal as creating products that infuse our daily lives with "joy" goes far beyond the usual sell of efficiency and style.

Some of the products were more successful than others, of course. In addition to the toilet brush, the teakettle and the toaster were big hits. But the Tripod line of frames and other objects never caught on. Around the Graves office, the line was jokingly called the "Sloth" for its three-toed shape and slow sales.

The Target teakettle was inevitably compared to the more expensive Alessi model. The Target version sold for a fraction of the price of the Alessi—although, Graves was always quick to point out, it

The game pieces in Graves' Monopoly set (2002) are miniature versions of products designed for Target.

Rethought and reboxed game classics such as Chinese checkers and dominoes became a whole line of Graves products at Target.

was built of the same gauge of steel. Alberto Alessi was irked, but he and Graves smoothed things over. "We are still working for Alessi and he has new, younger designers as well."

Five years after the first products were introduced, the original toaster still sells well, as do new products introduced every season. Graves' firm has won awards from the Industrial Designers Society of America, *I.D.* magazine, and the Chicago Athenaeum. In 2003 Target was honored with a National Design Award from the Smithsonian Institution for its commitment to the field. The relationship has redefined the public's expectations for design, as well as designers' perceptions. "Before the Graves-Target relationship, designers had no desire to work with a discounter," says Michael Francis, Target's executive vice president of marketing. "Now they all do."

But perhaps most importantly, by teaming with Target, Graves has achieved a goal that has eluded other designers for almost a century: bringing good design to a wide public. In the 1910s and 1920s the Wiener Werkstätte and the Bauhaus set out to combine craft and industry in a way that would bring well-designed goods to the masses. The same ideal was fostered by the Museum of Modern Art's "good design" program in the 1950s and by the Ulm School of Design in Germany in the 1950s and 1960s. But the prices never reached popular levels. "Certainly the Bauhaus dream was never realized, the idea of getting well-designed things to masses of people," Graves says. "The products were outrageously expensive."

Graves attributes these failings to the lack of a viable distribution network. "My take on this is that what is needed is somebody like Target in a big-box store with powerful distribution, marketing, and advertising that puts them in a position to get the price down. It is not even a matter of designer working closely with manufacturer. It is above all the distribution." Whether the delivery mechanism is the private automobile, railroads, or the Internet and UPS, the goal remains the same—to link designer and customer, and to improve individual lives with accessible design. ■

The early teakettles Graves designed for Alessi and Moller hardly exhausted his fund of teakettle ideas, as numerous versions have been created for Target.

Working drawing for Spinning Whistle teakettle

Below left: Electric teakettle, 2002

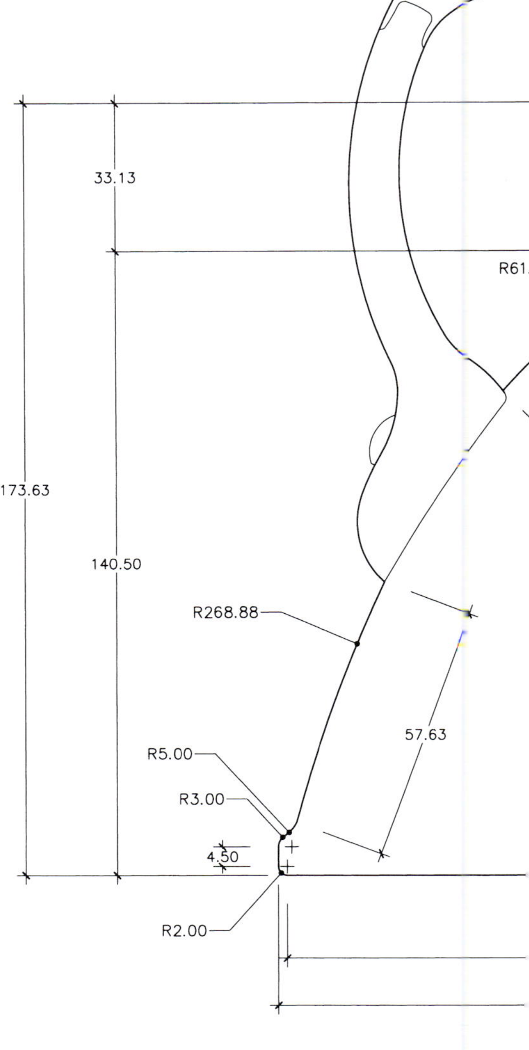

Coach's Whistle teakettle, 1999

Spinning Whistle teakettle, 2000

Left: In composing the facade of The Impala, a mixed-use residential tower on Manhattan's Upper East Side (1997), Graves created two-story window frames that relate in scale to both the individual dwelling units and the building as a whole, which appears smaller and more domestic as a result.

Right: Graves refers to his paintings, entitled "Archaic Landscapes," as a visual diary of elemental forms and compositions that can be utilized in buildings and products at many scales.

Landscapes," which depict fragments of archetypal forms in an imaginary landscape of fields and groves of trees. The forms are elemental and apply to architecture as well as to products—not literally, but because they are composed. The compositions are classical in approach, in that they "classify" the individual parts and relationships among them—for example, how the body of a building or a teakettle rests on its base. The plays on scale that occur are part of the language of architecture and design that we experiment with every day.

Diner toaster for Target, 2003

From Sketch Pad to Shopping Bag:
The Making of a Toaster

Every product begins as a concept, a flash of inspiration. Sometimes it is the designer who generates the idea; sometimes, the retailer sees a niche that needs to be filled. Graves had long wanted to make a toaster and had suggested a design for Alessi, but it was never produced.

At the first meeting with Graves and staff, Target immediately seized on the idea of a toaster as the signature product of the first Graves-Target collection. The toaster as a type spoke of families together at breakfast, and the freshness of a new day.

The toaster as a type spoke of families together at breakfast, and the freshness of a new day.

The toaster was an American invention and even an icon. One of the first appliances to be electrified by Thomas Edison and General Electric around the turn of the century, toasters had been produced in a variety of shapes over the years. The first home pop-up toaster, the Toastmaster Model 1-A-1, appeared in 1926. In the 1940s and 1950s, their variety echoed that of automobiles and radios.

According to historian Russell Flinchum, toaster technology was essentially mature by 1930. Design then became the critical differentiating element for competing models. The 1930s "Look while you cook" Birtman toaster offered a small window to watch the process. The 1940s continued the tradition of Streamlined-style chrome toasters. Later, "machine" toasters, such as the 1961 HT1 toaster for Braun, designed by Reinhold Weiss, took hold.

In 1995 Graves had designed a toaster for Alessi, who liked it enough to develop it through the prototype stage. Although Alessi later decided not to produce the toaster, the design was based on chrome quilting that recalled toasters of the 1930s.

Graves displays his first toaster and its companion blender (both 1999), manufactured by Black & Decker for Target, on the counter in his own kitchen in Princeton, New Jersey.

1 The toaster that Graves went on to create for Target was inspired by the Sunbeam toasters of the 1930s. That half-moon model had endured as an American archetype. Graves was familiar enough with it to include it in an illustration he did for a children's book written by humorist Fran Lebowitz and illustrated by Graves.

The Target design turned on its swelling shape, which Graves described as "blooming." The Sunbeam was, likewise, semicircular and suggested a sun rising above the horizon of the table—a neat evocation of breakfast as well as the company name. The Target toaster's shape was literally built up around the idea of "popping up." It bellowed upwards, as if it were holding its breath before expelling the toast. That gesture, that countertop anecdote, was the "story" of the toaster, expressed playfully in its silhouette.

Graves had long admired the Sunbeam toaster of the 1930s and used it in an illustration he made for Fran Lebowitz's children's book, *Mr. Chas and Lisa Sue Meet the Pandas*, published by Random House in 1994.

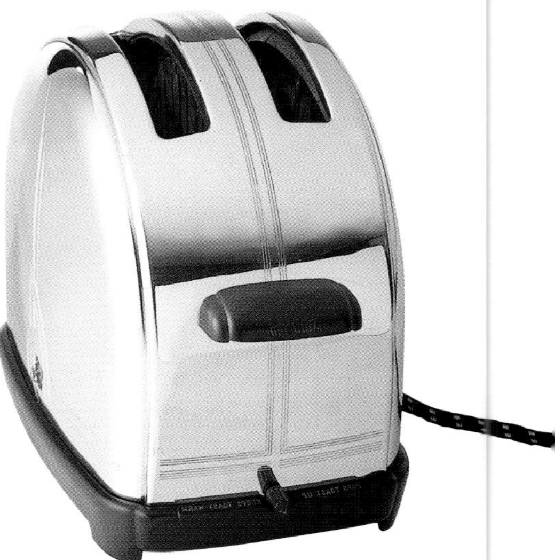

In 1995, Graves proposed a quilted aluminum and plastic toaster to Alessi, but the project never went forward.

Below: The initial idea for a product sometimes takes the form of a quick sketch on tracing paper.

The original Target toaster was playful, friendly, useful, and it came to sum up the line. Early ads for it bragged that it could be conveniently used "in the breakfast room," Graves' favorite space in his own house.

According to Donald Strum, the toaster exemplified a key Graves idea of creating a moment of heightened awareness that might cause its owner to take note of its presence. "We wanted the guest to go away with that shape indelibly etched in his mind. The forms that achieve such moments often go back to childhood and powerful impressions of the past," Strum explains. They are like folk rhymes or songs, archetypes, unconsciously picked up from books and films and previous experiences with products. The best product designs are something like a song heard on the radio that the listener can't get out of his head, an unforgettable melody.

2 That melody, however, had to be contained or framed in just the right proportions. "Michael is a master of proportions," says Strum. The desired form was worked out from Graves' first sketches in additional drawings and then in models. Several drawings were made of slightly wider and slightly higher toasters, to find just the right balance. To retain the "blooming" shape, it was important that the base of the body not be pulled in. It should be neither too tall nor too bulbous.

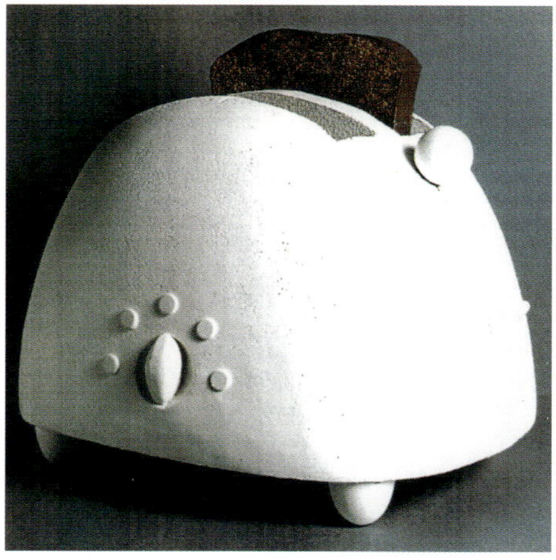

Left: The first study model for the toaster was roughed out quickly in a foam material that was coated with gesso and spray-painted. The second version added color.

Below: Once various technical issues were worked out with the manufacturer, a presentation model was made to show the final proportions and color.

3 Once the Graves team had proportions they were pleased with, a plain white model with no elaboration of detail and no indication of color was built of Styrofoam and presented to Target. After the client agreed to the overall shape, Graves' team went back to the studio to think about color.

It was at this stage that they landed on the color scheme that would inform all of the kitchen appliances in the series: blue for touch and yellow accents for dials. They also began to think about the user controls for the toaster: What kind of mechanism should be used to lower the bread into the heating elements? What kind of indicator and knob should control darkness?

4 As any design progresses, drawings become more technical. The designers use a combination of software. AutoCAD, a drafting program, produces exactly measured two-dimensional line drawings that can be easily transmitted to factories for shaping molds, dies, and other components for manufacturing. Rhino, a solid modeling program, turns the AutoCAD drawings into accurate, shaded, and highlighted renderings that suggest three dimensions. Rhino also allows colors and textures to be quickly changed on the screen. Throughout the process, the dedicated model shop that is a key part of Graves' office (and which builds not only all of the product models, but all of the architectural models as well) builds study models of dense foam or wood. Some are then painted to match the intended colors and surfaces.

5 The Target toaster presented certain practical challenges. Because of the short deadlines for the first collection, Graves had to design around an already existing Black & Decker chassis in order to get the toaster produced in time. When the first prototypes, which still used the semicircular, domed profile, were sent to Black & Decker's test labs in Connecticut, however, the top overheated. The metal slots through which the toast emerged were getting too hot. There was a danger of melting the plastic around the top opening, or chimney, as it was called. A flange was added to the metal slots to create small raised walls that would direct hot air upwards and away from the plastic.

In the end, the flanges were not enough, and the profile of the toaster had to be altered. The high arch gave way to a shape that suggests an exaggerated outline of a slice of bread. The high, central part of the arch was cut down into a lower, gentle undulation.

The working drawings produced by Graves' staff provide dimensional information to the manufacturer. The front view ghosts in how the inner workings fit within the exterior form of the toaster.

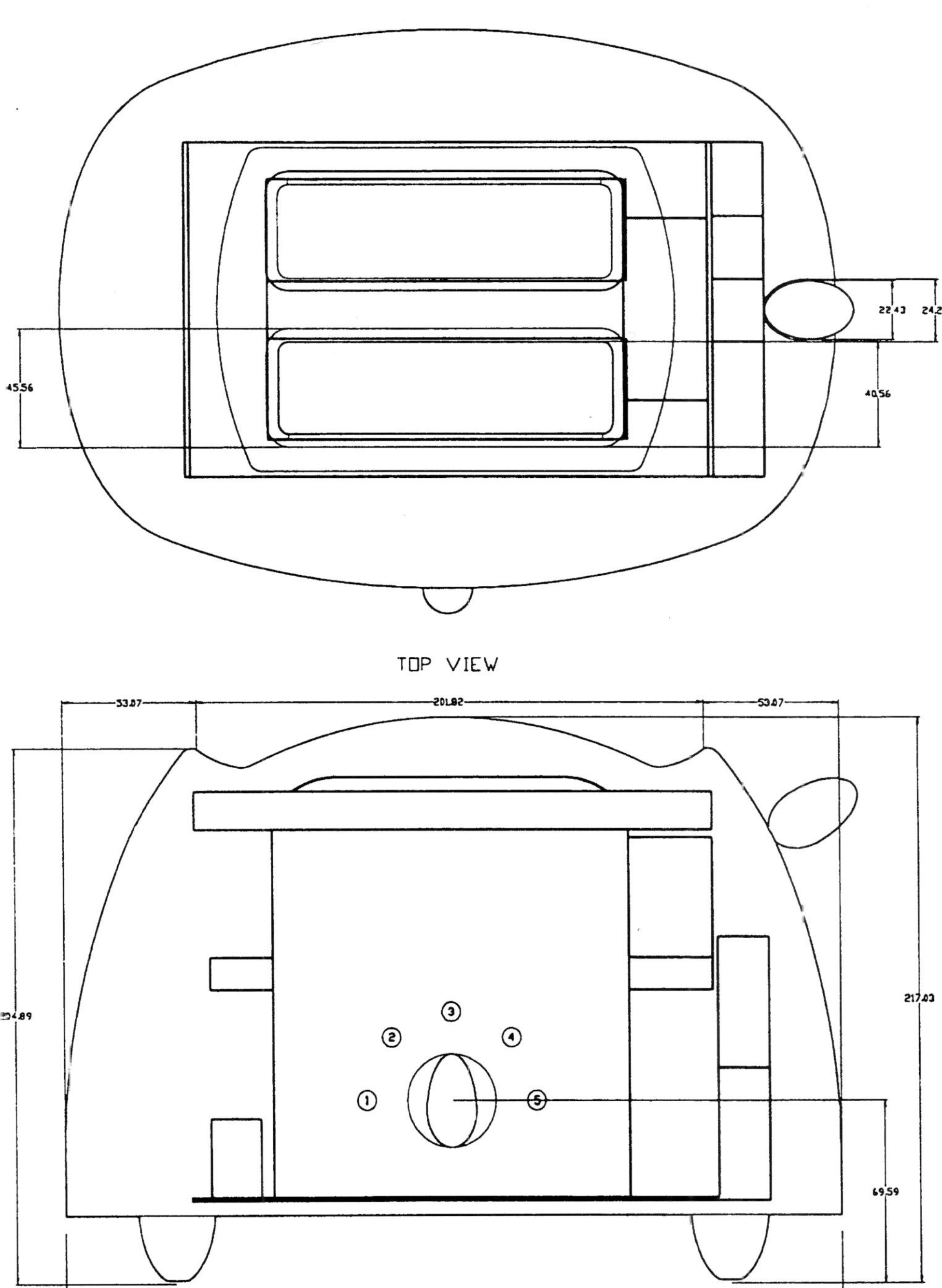

FRONT VIEW

A highly precise model is made as the basis for the mold used to produce the plastic body of the toaster.

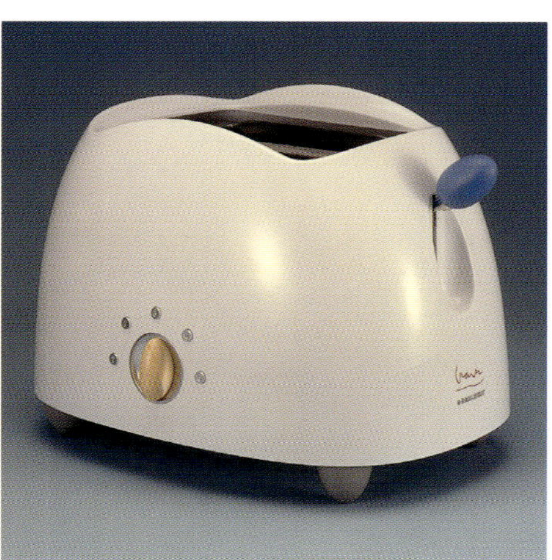

The final toaster, dubbed "pop art" and "toast modern" in Target ads, was one of the iconic pieces of the initial kitchen collection, introduced in 1999.

When manufacturing of the toaster began in China, other problems immediately surfaced. The handle for the control kept breaking. Designers from the Graves office and experts from Black & Decker were immediately dispatched to find a solution. "It always helps to be on the scene and talk to people face to face," says Strum. "We always like to visit the manufacturers, and we learn from the process." In this case, the answer was to strengthen the metal of the handle.

6 The user controls remained the same from early stages. The darkness control was five simple positions, light to dark, adjusted with a circular yellow dial. The blue egg-shaped knob on the end, for lowering bread to be toasted, was comfortable to hold, easy to operate, and became a touchstone for the entire collection.

Once any factory-line problems are solved, the full order of the product is manufactured. Designers like to see this stage, when their creation is rolling off the line and stacking up in the packing area.

7 The toaster starred in Target's ads for the Graves products. "toast modern" was one of the slogans used to promote the collection, and on buses and billboards the toaster, with toast popping out, was labeled "pop art." (In some of the first television ads Target did for the line, the toaster floated and spun, like a cartoon UFO.) An immediate success, the original toaster is still available, five years later, an undisputed champion in countertop appliances.

Black toaster, 2001

One year later, in 2000, the original white toaster was supplemented by a smaller black model. A wide-mouth model aimed at smaller kitchens, the black toaster had a different profile. It seemed to restrain the full body of the original with a belt around its waist. A flat blue curve emerged from the bottom of this model, a tab for tugging out and emptying the crumb tray. Making the handle oversized and bright, Donald Strum says, gave a humorous touch. "I call it celebrating the crumb tray."

For 2003, Graves created another toaster, a four-slice metal toaster with a wholly different outlook. The Diner toaster, aimed at a market for professional cookware that Target's trendwatchers had identified (those customers who might buy Viking or Wolf stoves and other professional cooking equipment), was done in stainless steel. It looked like a little Streamlined-style locomotive—or a roadside diner. The lines on its body made it look wider and lighter. Another early idea for this toaster used the quilted pattern associated with diners and with appliance cozies. The controls on the Target Diner toaster were modeled on the old rotary telephone—a theme used previously in clocks and wristwatches, where numbers appeared in round windows. Such a control was not just nostalgic, but familiar and welcoming. The egg shape of the control knob was toned down and reduced in size. The diner toaster, like its predecessors, has feet, and the stainless steel body swelled outward at four points to meet the feet of the plastic beneath, like fenders on a car.

Echoing the abundant designs available in the 1940s, Graves continues to create new toasters almost every year for Target. The most recent entry is a toaster oven in chrome, and more will surely follow. Toast may never go out of fashion, but some toasters do. ■

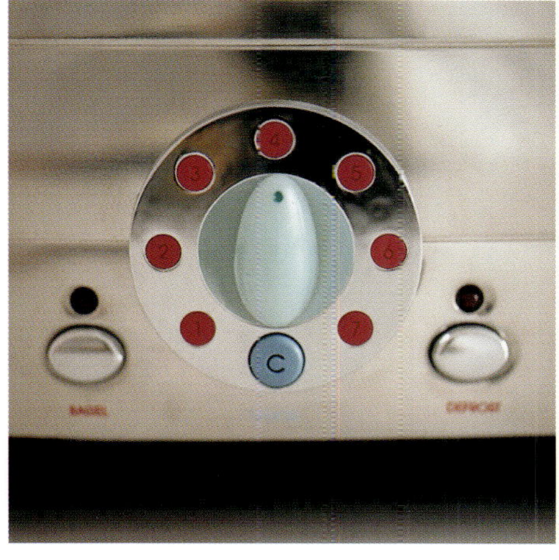

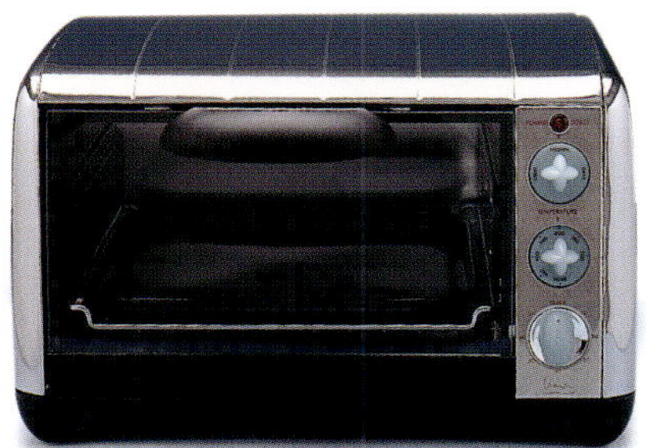

Above: Diner toaster, 2003

Left: Toaster oven, 2003

House and Home

Michael Graves Design Group gives new meaning to the word multidisciplinary, making literally everything a home might desire.

Twenty years have passed since Michael Graves drafted plans for the Humana Building in Louisville, Kentucky, a project that set the designer squarely on course to combine—under one holistic discipline—architecture, interiors, and objects for the home and office. It also has been twenty years since Alessi introduced the Tea and Coffee Piazza that was Graves' springboard into the world of product design. And in early 2004, Michael Graves and Target Stores celebrate the fifth anniversary of a landmark collaboration that has brought good design to households across the nation.

These three milestones point to the roads by which Graves has arrived at his position as a pioneer of the new American home. The country is today fascinated by all things designed, with a capital "D." A new level of sophistication informs consumers' choices in everything from forks to furniture. In recent years, Graves has become as well known in the public eye for artful objects as for buildings, thereby helping to redefine the role of architects. While many modernist designers created exquisite home furnishings, beginning with Le Corbusier and Ludwig Mies van der Rohe in the

Top: Target placed clever pop-up ads featuring the Brighton Pavilion in several magazines during the summer of 2003.

Above: Graves' sketch and a computer rendering of the Heathcote Pavilion manufactured by Lindal Cedar Homes and available through target.com, 2003

1920s, few have done so with the range and versatility of Graves. Even fewer have done it with the same popular success—Alessi has sold some two million of his whistling bird teakettles. His collaboration with Target, now totaling nearly eight hundred distinct objects, continues to thrive and innovate in new areas. For its role in promoting good design via the product lines created by its talented designer partners such as Graves, Target received a National Design Award from the Smithsonian's Cooper-Hewitt, National Design Museum in 2003, the first time a retailer has been so honored. Two years earlier, Graves' peers in the American Institute of Architects

Top: Graves' rendering demonstrated how the octagonal Brighton Pavilion can be added to the kit home called Maybeck.

Above left: A 2,000-square-foot house designed by Graves using pre-cut parts made by Lindal Cedar Homes was a sweepstakes prize for Target's "Club Wedd" bridal registry.

Above right: Michael Graves Design Group became an independent company in 2003, with its own logo.

bestowed on him their highest honor, the Gold Medal, saying that Graves' "art delights in the pleasure of living, inviting the public, not as an observer or even a guest, but as a participant in his joyous celebration of life."

Since Michael Graves Design Group became an independent company within the larger practice in 2003, its mandate has been best summed up by a saying often invoked at the studio: "The house and everything in it." This catchphrase indicates the ambitious and comprehensive vision of Graves' designers—that all buildings and the objects within them are parts of a unified whole. Viewing domestic design as a seamless and complete process, from exterior wall to interior countertop, the Design Group gives new meaning to the word multidisciplinary, making literally everything a home might desire. New and forthcoming products include rugs and carpets for Glen Eden, furniture for the David Edward Company, a signature collection of kitchen and tabletop items for Dansk, and architectural products for Delta Faucet and Progress Lighting.

This Graves' kit home, called Downing, pays homage to early American country cottages like those of Andrew Jackson Downing.

The Design Group is even taking major steps to merge product design and architecture, proposing ways to sell good architecture much like a teakettle or toaster. Small buildings that Graves calls Pavilions were offered for sale on Target's website, beginning in 2003. With Gary Lapera, a partner in the firm, Graves designed a line of customized single rooms that can stand free as a pavilion, connect to an existing house, or be joined to another Graves structure. To Graves, these rooms symbolize domestic lifestyle choices. "Imagine sitting in one of these in your backyard at sunset, reading, with a glass of wine in your hand," he says. "It would be amazing."

He and Lapera also envision streamlining the process of home renovation, often so painful and disruptive as to be discouraging. Similar to buying a book on Amazon.com, customers can purchase extra living space over the Internet with a few clicks of their mouse. From a menu of options, they first decide if the Pavilion is to be attached to their existing house or will be freestanding, then choose a basic shape—square, rectangle, or octagon—and finally the type and color of the roof and siding. The Pavilions are delivered in parts and assembled on site by the manufacturer, Seattle-based Lindal Cedar Homes.

Graves' studio is also designing a series of kits for complete homes—not just pavilions—that can be bought and customized using a similar process. Its public debut is being awarded as the grand prize of a sweepstakes for Target's popular bridal registry, "Club Wedd." Many of the soon-to-be-wed who register at Target choose Graves' products, so the retailer wanted to give away a starter

For Dansk, long an exemplar of Danish modernism, Graves was commissioned to create a signature collection that infuses the company's tradition of purity of form with a bit of attitude. The challenge was to reinterpret classic mid-twentieth-century modern as it is appreciated at the beginning of the twenty-first century. The Graves designers emphasized basic forms but rendered them slightly oversized and often with a new angle, suggesting a fresh perspective—and sometimes a touch of wit.

Ellington lounge chair for the David Edward Company, 2003

home, to be built anywhere in the country, designed by Graves himself. It's a classic Graves-Target collaboration. "At what other store could you register for tableware and end up with a new home by a world-famous architect?" remarked Lapera.

The Club Wedd house became a prototype for the series. Because the identity of the winners and the location of the house would be unknown for some time, Graves realized that the best way to fulfill the commission was to work with a manufacturer such as Lindal Cedar Homes, which supplies kits for wood-frame houses all over the country. The Club Wedd house was designed with flexible components to meet the taste of the winners and the demands of the location. "We are working with Lindal's existing post-and-beam construction system, but are devising a new vocabulary of parts," says Lapera. "We think of it as a chassis you can accessorize."

The domestic character of the line of houses that will be built from these kits is just as important to Graves as the delivery system. Unlike many earlier approaches to modular or prefabricated housing, which tend toward the boxiness of an industrial shipping container, the Graves homes project a clear domestic aura. They are all two stories under a bold, angled roof—a primal, sheltering shape ubiquitous in children's house drawings. As with some of the Pavilions, particularly those with bracketed roofs, the houses recall American country cottages like those of the much-loved nineteenth-century architect Andrew Jackson Downing, to whom Graves has paid homage by naming one of the houses "Downing."

The houses' plans, which center on a living space called a "great room," can be adapted to many environments. "You can make choices in the uses of the rooms based on your lifestyle, and you can locate the house to suit your site," says Lapera. "We are asking both, 'Which of your activities need space?' and 'Where do you want the sun to come up?'" The designs also allow for logical additions, such as extra bedrooms or a home office, which can take the form of Michael Graves Pavilions.

The results of all this planning are houses that can be sold in a manner like the Pavilions and constructed anywhere in the country. The designs represent an attempt to achieve that long-cherished and frequently frustrated American dream of reasonably priced, well-designed houses for everyone, pioneered by Sears'

Graves has designed a new line for the David Edward Company, an American contemporary furniture maker based in Baltimore. The wood and upholstered Hampton lounge chair (left) achieved a special design success. The sturdiness of the arms created support and easy access for people with disabilities, attracting interest from the health care industry.

Above: Models for the David Edward Company, 2003

Right: Hampton side chair for the David Edward Company, 2003

Rug maker Glen Eden's unique manufacturing process makes it possible to employ different heights of wool within a single woven rug. The patterns of Graves' designs for the company use that process to play with scale. Decorative motifs from traditional oriental rugs are taken out of their original context and blown up to serve as the vocabulary of the new rugs. Traditional elements remain, but when their scale is changed, they also become modern.

pre–World War II kit homes and, in a different way, by the Case Study House program of the 1950s, in which noted designers such as Charles and Ray Eames and Pierre Koenig designed simple homes as examples of how modern architecture could work for domestic environments.

This bold plan for the residential market has the potential to do for domestic architecture what Graves has already done for domestic products. "We want to meld architecture and design," says partner Karen Nichols. "The American suburban home, ranging from dreary McMansions to tract houses, is in desperate need of reinvention."

Meanwhile, Graves continues to create new products for Target, at the rate of nearly a hundred each year. In Target Stores, Graves enjoys the status of something like a sub-brand, with creations found in many departments. Home decor—which includes kitchenware, decorative accessories, and games—is the mainstay, along with cleaning supplies and lawn and garden products. However, special programs place Graves' products all over the store, with memorable objects created for the home office, telephones and electronics, "soft lines" such as bedding and curtains, jewelry and watches, and even framed art.

"For our guests, Michael Graves stands for design," says Target's Michael Francis. "We consider him our dean of design. He continues to create exciting products for Target and has paved the way for our other designer partnerships." Target now also works with designers such as Isaac Mizrahi, Mossimo Giannulli, Cynthia Rowley, and Karim Rashid. The Graves relationship, however, was not only the first for Target—it remains unique. Graves enjoys a status approaching house designer, called on by the company for out-of-the-box projects. As with the Washington Monument restoration that started the relationship, the Target-Graves collaboration has been especially

Above: With arcing, exuberant curves and ellipsoid handles set at jaunty angles, a collection for Delta Faucet features finishes such as matte chrome with translucent handles.

Following pages: Michael Graves' own kitchen is a site for ongoing experimentation with ideas of domesticity. He outfits it with products that inspire him as well as his own designs, including a new kitchen faucet and handle set for Delta Faucet prior to its market debut in 2004.

Target products designed for 2004 include an innovative gooseneck desk lamp (right) and such kitchen products as a salad spinner and a bagel slicer.

effective in arts and education including philanthropic endeavors like an outdoor performance venue at Harriet Island Park in St. Paul, Minnesota, and an elephant fountain at St. Jude Children's Research Hospital in Memphis. Target's widespread support of the arts led to the sponsorship of the New York run of a major traveling museum exhibition on recent American design, for which Graves' studio conducted public lectures and participated in a design symposium.

Today, the ripple effect of design's influence on the retail world has helped to create a new consumer culture. Recognizing the value of Graves' work for Target, other discounters have converted to the faith, asking designers to add presence to their common products. For top executives, designers are increasingly seen as the force that makes brands vital and helps them grow. Even the most jaded accountants take note of the impact of design as manifest in, for example, the reinvention of luxury stalwart Gucci under Tom Ford. The sea change has led to the new term—gawky but useful—"masstige," slang for prestige items for the mass market. This means applying design in unfamiliar areas, resulting in products that are perceived as celebrities—the Apple iPod, the new Mini Cooper automobile, and Graves' toilet brush. But, in a sense, all are descendents of Graves' iconic Alessi whistling bird teakettle.

Michael Graves Design Group's new work builds on the approaches and values that it has accumulated over the years. Key among them is the drive to give the form and function of each object such memorable presence that it creates a moment of what members of the Graves team refer to as "heightened awareness"—with the larger goal of deepening the quality of life itself. Just as ordinary tools, thought through and reinvented, become extraordinary products, daily routine, examined and celebrated, becomes ritual. The ordinary becomes extraordinary. And this process makes it possible to examine and visually articulate all the elements of domestic living.

The shapes of homes and everything in them are always expressions of the values by which we live. Michael Graves' designs imply a world in which every task is to be savored. For him, design for everyday living is nothing less than designing life every day. ■

Above: The House at Indian Hill near Cincinnati, Ohio (1996), includes dramatic interiors furnished with numerous Graves-designed products.

Right: Graves' breakfast room table becomes a convivial setting with garden-inspired Deanrey china and crystal salt and pepper shakers, designed for Alessi in 1992.

Following pages: Graves designed a showhouse known as Cedar Gables for the 1999 Minneapolis-area Parade of Homes. It was outfitted with furniture, furnishings, and artwork designed by the firm, along with the just-introduced line of products for Target, fulfilling the ongoing dream of designing "the house and everything in it."

Index

Page numbers in bold indicate images.

Above: Whistling bird teakettle for Alessi, 1985

Acknowledgments

We are indebted to the staffs of Michael Graves Design Group and Michael Graves & Associates. Special thanks are due to Courtney Havran for assistance with images and to Venina Tandela and Mary Jo Mitchell for consultation on graphics. For their time and support, we are grateful to Michael Graves and Karen Nichols, as well as the other principals, Gary Lapera, Patrick Burke, John Diebboll, Tom Rowe, and Susan Howard. The help of the senior staff, Linda Kinsey and Donald Strum, and the studio heads, Eric Bogner, Bill Harrington, and David Peschel, is much appreciated.

Our thanks are also due to David Brown, John Meils, Lia Ronnen, Lindsey Stanberry, Shoshana Thaler, and Megan Worman at Melcher Media; Sunnie Guglielmo and Michael Bierut at Pentagram; Matthew Septimus, Jen Everett, Amanda Thompson, and Max Dickstein.

Credits

All images appear courtesy of Michael Graves & Associates (photos by George Kopp) unless otherwise noted below.

Photos by Matthew Septimus: pages 10 (top), 18 (top), 50 (bottom), 51 (bottom), 57-61, 62 (bottom), 63 (top), 64-65 (top), 66-69, 80, 87 (top), 91 (top), 93, 96 (left), 97, 103, 106 (right), 108 (top), 109 (bottom right), 114, 127

Page 11: "Model 302" telephone, 1937, designed by Henry Dreyfuss. Cooper-Hewitt, National Design Museum, Smithsonian Institution. The Decorative Arts Association Acquisitions Fund, 1994-73-2. Photo: Hiro Ihara.

14 right: "Petipoint" Iron, 1941, designed by Brooks Stevens. Milwaukee Art Museum, Purchase, with funds from Barbara and Wallace Lee, John Terry Brown, Jr., and Elizabeth and Samuel Greeley in memory of James Brachman.

16-17: *Entrance to the Zephyr*, by Otto Perry. Photo courtesy Denver Public Library.

19: Wall clock, c. 1949, designed by George Nelson & Associates. Cooper-Hewitt, National Design Museum, Smithsonian Institution. Gift of Mel Byars, 1991-26-1. Photo: Victor Schrager.

21 bottom: Taylor Photo

22: Copyright Peter Aaron/Esto

23: Taylor Photo

24 top: Photo: Chas McGrath. Courtesy Sunar.

29 left and right: Timothy Hursley

31 bottom and 36-37: Courtesy Alessi

41 left: John Donat

41 right: Susan Gilmore Photography

45 right: Courtesy Duravit

71 top: John Donat

73: Copyright Paul Irmiter. Courtesy Target.

81 bottom: Risa Korris

94 and 95 top left and bottom right: James Wojcik

95 top right and bottom left: Earl Kendall

100: Jud Haggard

101 left: Norman McGrath

104 top: Sunbeam "Silent Automatic" Toaster, 1938, designed by George T. Scharfenberg. Cooper-Hewitt, National Design Museum, Smithsonian Institution. The Decorative Arts Association Acquisitions Fund, 1993-150-43. Photo: Dave King.

115, 116 bottom left and right: Courtesy David Edward Company

120-21: Courtesy Delta Faucet

123 top: Courtesy Scott Frances/*Architectural Digest*

124-25: Susan Gilmore Photography

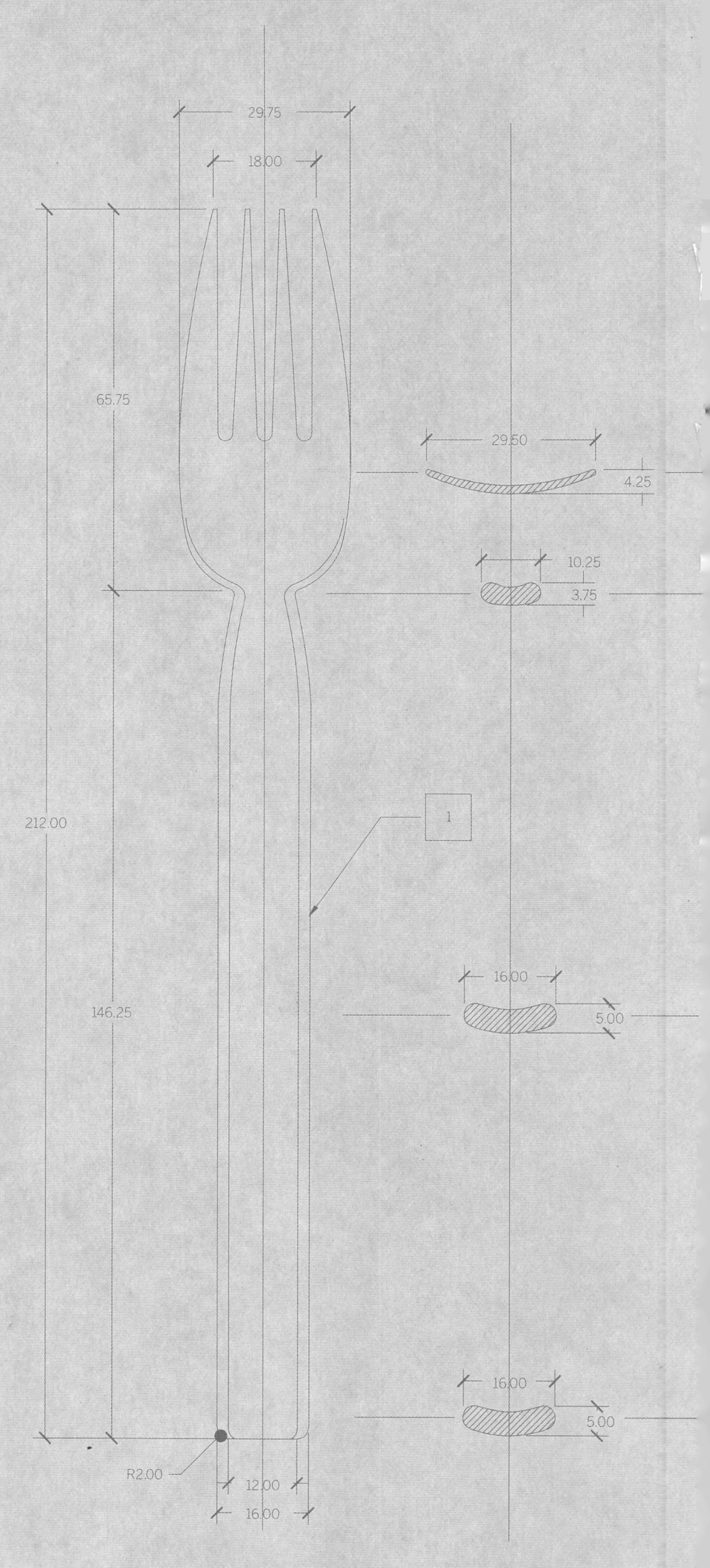

29.75
18.00
65.75
212.00
146.25
29.50
4.25
10.25
3.75
1
16.00
5.00
16.00
5.00
R2.00
12.00
16.00